DISCOVER
CORNWALL

DISCOVER CORNWALL

20 walks to explore the county

Sue Kittow

Published by Sigma Leisure – an imprint of
Sigma Press, Stobart House, Pontyclerc, Penybanc Road, Ammanford, Carmarthenshire SA18 3HP.

British Library Cataloguing in Publication Data
A CIP record for this book is available from the British Library.

ISBN: 978-1-85058-928-0

Typesetting and Design by: Sigma Press, Ammanford.

Cover photograph: Coombe Creek © Claire Wilson

Maps: © Bute Cartographics

photographs: © Claire Wilson and Sue Kittow

Printed by: TJ International Ltd, Padstow, Cornwall

Contents

To Pip
Who was always waiting at the other end

Locations of walks

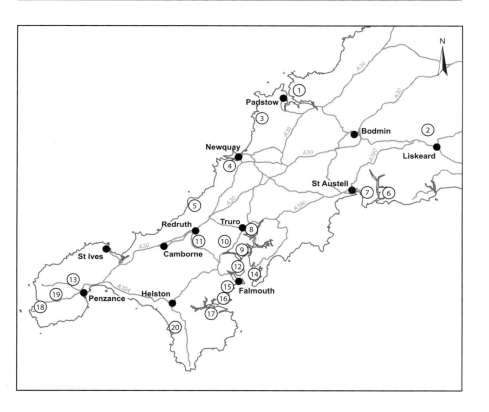

Introduction to Cornwall

Cornwall has been a popular holiday destination with the upper classes since the time of Henry VIII, but developed as a tourist destination during Victorian times when it became fashionable to go to the seaside, and towns such as Newquay changed from being a fishing village into a popular resort. Tourism now makes up a large part of Cornwall's economy, but it does place a lot of price pressure on local houses, especially as wages are below the national average. Cornwall's stunning scenery, charm and mild climate ensure a continual interest and loyalty from all who visit.

Cornwall's fine golden sands have provided the backdrop for many childhood holidays, but it is also a wonderful county to explore on foot. As well as the coastal footpath, there are numerous less known routes that it has been great fun to investigate.

The north and south coasts of Cornwall are very different in nature: the north, facing the Atlantic Ocean is more exposed and much wilder, with a dramatic coastline, but it also has many extensive stretches of golden sands.

The south coast, sometimes known as the "Cornish Riviera", is more sheltered with several estuaries offering popular and safe anchorages, as in Falmouth and Fowey. The south coast beaches tend to be of coarser sand and shingle but the many fishing villages such as Polperro and Looe are equally as popular with tourists.

The walks in this book vary in length but as many people do not have the luxury of time for long walks, the selection has been kept to 4 to 6 miles in length and the walks are suitable for most capabilities though some are more taxing than others. At the beginning of each walk is a factbox giving information on the walk.

When walking, it is advisable to wear appropriate footwear and clothing, take food, water, and first aid as well as maps and a compass. In many parts of Cornwall, mobile phones don't work so make sure you plan your route before you go and let others know when and where you are walking.

Livestock frequently graze near public footpaths so please put dogs on leads and treat animals cautiously and with respect.

Please take rubbish home with you. Keep dogs under control at all times, particularly near the cliff edge. Dogs are liable to chase rabbits or birds over the edge, so keep them on leads in such places.

Take care on country roads, and please shut all gates after you have passed through them.

Maps used for these walks are the Ordinance Survey Explorer series.

1. Daymer Bay and Rock

A walk in Betjeman country taking in "one of the best beaches in the world"

Daymer Bay is a good sized beach in North Cornwall, bordered by dunes and sandhills, about a mile south of Polzeath. Compared to the open sands of Polzeath and Rock, Daymer Bay is more secluded: the fine pale sandy beach is within the mouth of the Camel Estuary so is pretty sheltered and has a gently sloping beach making it safe for swimming.

At the southern end of the beach is Bray Hill, a grassy mound from the top of which are wonderful views of the area. At the foot of the hill, a little way from the beach, is St Enodoc Church, which is where the former Poet Laureate, John Betjeman is buried. This church is also known as Sinking Neddy because of its proximity to the sea and sand.

The original name of Rock, recorded in the 14th century, was Blaketore, or Black Tor. By the 18th Century this had become Black Rock and is now the name of the ferry that operates between Rock and Padstow. However, the name has been shortened to Rock. Recently, Rock has become known as 'Britain's Saint-Tropez' and the 'Kensington of Cornwall' because of the very rich upper class who tend to holiday here. Rock is just inside the Camel Estuary opposite Padstow and home to a wide variety of boats – Rock Sailing Club's headquarters in a converted warehouse on a wharf is a local landmark. Rock is also home to Sharp's Brewery, a very popular

Distance	3 miles
Time	1½ - 2 hours
Terrain	Easy walking but can be steep over the sand dunes
Car park and public toilets	Daymer Bay and Quarry car park, Rock
Passenger ferry	From Rock to Padstow below the Rock Inn, near Quarry car park
Refreshments	Café at Daymer Bay summer only; café and pubs at Rock
Map	Explorer 106 Newquay and Padstow

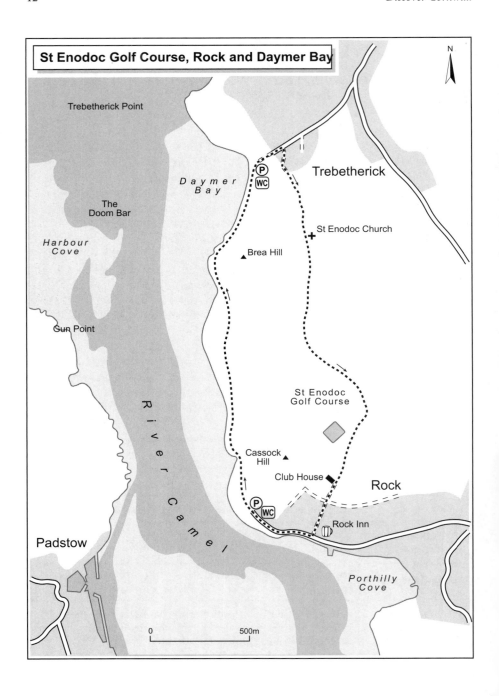

St Enodoc Golf Course, Rock and Daymer Bay

N

Trebetherick Point

D a y m e r
B a y

P
WC

Trebetherick

The
Doom Bar

St Enodoc Church

Harbour
Cove

▲ Brea Hill

Gun Point

*R
i
v
e
r*

*C
a
m
e
l*

St Enodoc
Golf Course

Cassock
Hill ▲

Club House

Rock

P
WC

Rock Inn

Padstow

Porthilly
Cove

0   500m

Daymer Bay

independent real ale brewery established in the mid 1990s. This walk was done on a mild day in December.

The Walk

From Wadebridge, take the B3314 signposted to Rock and Polzeath. Several miles on turn left to Rock and Pityme, and just past the Pityme Inn take a small turning on the right to Polzeath. After about a mile is a dusty sign on the left for Daymer Bay. This lane is steep and narrow and leads down to a public car park at Daymer Bay where there is a shop open in summer and public toilets open all year round.

Walk back up the lane a few yards and turn right, down a private road signposted Footpath to St Enodoc Church. There are large houses on either side, one of which was owned by John Betjeman, who spent many happy times here. This path leads to the windswept golf course of St Enodoc.

A path indicated by white painted stones leads to the minute church of St Enodoc, the last resting place of John Betjeman, and also of Fleur

St Enodoc Church

Lombard, the first female firefighter to die on duty in peacetime Britain. The tiny Norman church, with its wonderfully crooked spire, was buried in the sand dunes for many years and the vicar had to be lowered into the church through a skylight to take the annual service. In 1863 the Reverend Hart Smith started to restore this "sinkininny" church which is still without electricity, but much loved both as a worship place and a shrine for Betjeman followers.

The door is often beautifully decorated with holly, and a pot of rosemary stands to one side of the entrance; a pot of white heather on the other side. A notice advises that the church is open from 0730 to dusk, and inside are sometimes bouquets of pungent lilies at the door. This church, cradled in a sand dune and surrounded by tamarisk trees, is a peaceful oasis in the desert of modern life.

Back on the golf course, more white stones guide round the side of the greens, with an overgrown valley and stream to the right; presumably the same stream that Betjeman dammed as a boy while acting as a grudging caddy for his father.

Follow a sign to the left, over a bridge built "in memory of Tom Regis", and more white painted stones dotted over the undulating greens, which head towards the sand dunes. This path leads to the golf club car park, and down the hill into Rock and the Rock Inn, useful for a quick drink. The view from the pub is spectacular: in winter the slate green Camel Estuary is sprinkled with empty moorings like hundreds and thousands. Padstow sprawls opposite, with Prideaux Place behind, and the Rock to Padstow passenger ferry trundles back and forth.

Continue on to the Quarry car park (more public toilets here if you need them) and walk back along the path that meanders through the sand dunes. If the tide is out, walk back along the beach but make sure of tide times: this is a particularly treacherous part of the coast. The path through the sand dunes leads over knotted roots rubbed bare by countless feet, and passes winter hawthorn that looks as if it had been sprayed with golden lichen.

Over to the left is Harbour Cove and Hawker's Cove and, further on, Stepper Point and the lookout station. Doom Bar is visible over the Camel Estuary, with waves rippling on the sandbank. According to legend, this

View from St Enodoc Golf Course

was the curse of a mermaid shot by a sailor: shortly after her death a great storm threw up the sandbank and wrecked many ships in the harbour. Doom Bar has wrecked over 600 ships since records began 200 years ago.

Walking round the headland, below is the wide expanse of Daymer Bay, which has changed little in the last fifty years. No wonder the Sunday Times featured this as one of the six best beaches in the world: it's perfect for small children playing on the beach but equally good for surfing and water sports.

2. Golitha Falls and King Doniert's Stone

A walk through a wooded valley, then climb up for wonderful views over Bodmin Moor

Golitha Falls, on the edge of Bodmin Moor, is an ancient and mystical place where it feels as if anything could happen. Apparently, when a full moon is shining, you can catch a glimpse of 'Golitha', the Old Man of the woods. Golitha is actually pronounced 'Goleetha', meaning 'obstruction' in Cornish. King Doniert (or Dunrgarth) was one of Cornwall's last Kings, who was drowned while hunting in the River Fowey (pronounced Foye) at Golitha Falls in the year AD875.

This walk was done on a freezing day in February.

Distance	1½ - 2 hours
Time	Approximately 2½ miles
Terrain	Walking near the falls is uneven with lots of tree roots, though the first part is suitable for wheelchairs. The walk up through the woods is steep in places, and can be very muddy. Be careful near the river with young children and dogs
Public toilets	Golitha Falls car park
Refreshments	None
Map	OS Explorer 109 Bodmin Moor

The Walk

Heading up the A390, turn left onto the B3360 to Doublebois, cross over the A38 and continue until reaching the hamlet of Redgate. Take the lane on the left and after a quarter of a mile cross over Draynes Bridge. Beyond that is the Golitha Falls National Nature Reserve, and opposite a large car park with some public toilets that are closed in winter. Cross over the road and set off through the woods towards Golitha Falls.

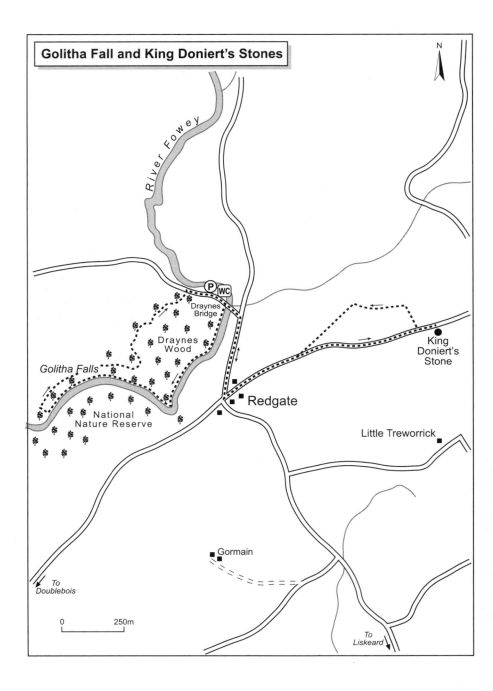

Golitha Fall and King Doniert's Stones

River Fowey

P WC

Draynes
Bridge

Draynes
Wood

Golitha Falls

King
Doniert's
Stone

National
Nature Reserve

Redgate

Little Treworrick

To
Doublebois

Gormain

To
Liskeard

0   250m

Woods at Golitha Falls

There are various footpaths leading through these woods along the banks of the River Fowey where the beech trees are covered in a thick green moss, like hot water bottle covers, though the moss is apparently lichen and a sign of pure air. The trees are protected by a Tree Preservation Order and are a relic of the ancient woodland that once covered much of the surrounding area. There are several abandoned mine workings here, some of which are home to bats such as the noctule, brown long-eared and lesser horseshoe. Many varieties of birds have been recorded here, including buzzard, dipper, nuthatch and treecreeper. And if you visit in warmer times, all kinds of moths and butterflies can be seen, including the silver-washed fritillary.

Follow one of the many footpaths that climb up the hillside and look down to get a better view of how the Fowey River passes over a series of cascades for over eight hundred yards. The falls look magical with the sun sparkling on the pounding waterfalls against a backdrop of moss covered boulders. Climbing up, notice an extraordinary tree, again covered in lichen, with clumps of little twigs sprouting from it like baby hedgehogs.

Golitha Falls

Join a higher path which winds through abandoned mine workings and eventually back to the car park. From here, walk over Draynes Bridge, which was built for pack horses in the 15th century. At the end of this road turn left at a T-junction and climb up the steep road until reaching King Doniert's Stones, which have been set in a walled off area to the right of the road. The Doniert stones are parts of early mediaeval crosses made from local granite, richly carved and dating back to the 9th century. The shorter stone carries a Latin inscription which translates as "Doniert ordered this cross for the good of his soul".

There are incredible views over the moors from the stones – the village of St Cleer lies to the left, the church spire dominating the clutch of houses, and The Crows Nest pub is recommended at nearby Darite.

For the return journey, pass through a gate a few yards down the road on the right which traverses rough moorland, pockmarked with hoof, paw and footprints. The lichen here is even more dramatic, dripping from the branches like ghostly grey beards. On the right is a quarry, into which whole trees have fallen, and a pond on the left, covered in thick emerald weed.

From here turn left at a junction of several paths and head back through a gate leading back to the road and retrace your steps back along the road, arriving back at the car park.

Other local place of interest

Nearby Siblyback Lake is one of Cornwall's main reservoirs and a popular watersports and recreation centre.

3. Bedruthan Steps and Park Head

Spectacular cliff top views make this one of the most popular walks on the Cornish coast

Coastal erosion has worn back the cliff face around Bedruthan Steps leaving huge outcrops of volcanic rock scattered along the length of the beach. These towering monoliths are surrounded by water at high tide, but at low tide there is approximately a mile of beach surrounding them. The massive scale of these rocks gives the beach, cliffs and surrounding scenery an almost magical feeling that is well worth experiencing. This walk was done on a hot August day.

Distance	3 miles
Time	2 hours
Terrain	Steep in parts, can be slippery when wet, and keep well away from the cliff edge
Refreshments	Carnewas Shop and Café: Tel 01637 860701 to check for opening times or email: carnewas@nationaltrust.org
Map	OS Explorer 106 Newquay and Padstow
Car park	At Bedruthan Steps, £2 at time of walking

The Walk

To get there, take the B3276 coast road from Newquay going through Mawgan Porth. Ignoring the sign to Bedruthan Steps and car park, continue until a small green sign on the left indicates Pentire Farm and Park Head. A few yards up the lane park in a (free) National Trust car park on the right hand side.

Head up the lane, signposted Porth Mear (ignoring footpath on the left to Pentire Steps and Park Head). Before Pentire Farm, take a footpath sign on the right to Porth Mear and Park Head, over a step stile next to a farm gate and into a large field.

View of Bedruthan Steps from the clifftop

One of the giant boulders

Following a garden wall, walk diagonally left across the field past another stile into another field and continue until reaching a kissing gate on the left at the very bottom of the field, leading into a valley. There are boardwalks here for wetter times and in summer there are foxgloves, ragged robin, dog roses and cow parsley, and a profusion of honeysuckle. Some of this is lemon scented, others smell of honey, others give a really pungent sweet smell like hot butterscotch.

This part of the walk is scratchy on the legs and populated with waist high nettles and nutty smelling bracken, so trousers are advised rather than shorts. Continue through the valley until reaching a fast flowing stream on the right that leads to Porth Mear beach which looks like a lunar landscape with boulders strewn everywhere.

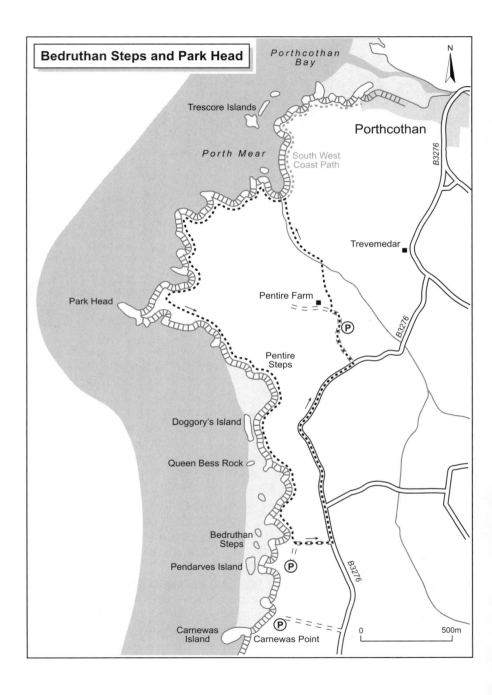

Bedruthan Steps and Park Head

Porthcothan Bay

Trescore Islands

Porthcothan

Porth Mear

South West Coast Path

Trevemedar

Park Head

Pentire Farm

Pentire Steps

Doggory's Island

Queen Bess Rock

Bedruthan Steps

Pendarves Island

Carnewas Island

Carnewas Point

B3276

N

0   500m

Climb the coastal path to the left of the cove, passing a National Trust sign to Park Head and go through another kissing gate with a map and a red spot indicating 'You Are Here'. The coastal path veers round to the left around several coves and in summer the only sound is the cheerful song of skylarks. At this time of year the ground is smothered in Common Bird's Foot Trefoil, the cliffs covered in perpendicular rabbit holes, and the views are stunning – Dinas Head and Trevose Lighthouse shine in the far distance, and nearer, the golden sands of Constantine Bay shimmer in the glory of low tide.

After a short piece of stone wall, take the right fork of a path which leads to a small stone memorial which apparently was commemorated to the person who donated the land to the National Trust, although there were no signs to indicate this. Walking out over the headland find the remains of a ditch and rampart, once part of the fortification of an Iron Age cliff castle.

Return to the memorial and veer right along the coastal path. Further on a kissing gate leads back to the car park, but ignore this and carry on, through another kissing gate with Pentire Steps far below.

At another stone wall with a tamarisk hedge growing out of the top, pause and admire the view. On the other side of the hedge, the sea sighs like the swishing of a long dress, and a heat haze shimmers above the ground.

Park Head cliffs

Porth Mear

The views are breathtaking. Looking west is Newquay Bay with mile after mile of postcard perfection. To the right are more humps which form the remains of earthworks designed to protect Redcliff Castle, thousands of years ago.

Bedruthan Steps gets its name from the huge slate rocks scattered along the beach, rather than the almost vertical man made steps leading down to the beach. Legend has it that the giant Bedruthan used the boulders as stepping stones, for at low tide the beach is over a mile long with many wonderful rock pools and caves. However, the cliffs are highly dangerous and many people have been cut off on the beach at high tide: there are warnings against swimming here at any time.

A steep staircase, recently rebuilt by the National Trust, leads down to the beach, so do not undertake this if you are unwell or unfit. The steps are extremely steep and often wet and slippery. The gate providing access to the steps is locked between November and February.

To complete the walk, either walk back along the road or retrace steps to the kissing gate at Pentire Steps which leads back to the car park.

4. Polly Joke

A coastal walk taking in Polly Joke beach, West Pentire and Cubert Common

The West Pentire headland is sandwiched between two beautiful and unspoiled beaches: Crantock and Porth "Polly" Joke. The coastal footpath provides a circular walk of the headland, where you can see the wildness of the Atlantic Ocean, watch seabirds at play and wander through poppy and rape seeded fields. This area has become very popular for campers and surfers over recent years, and is still a good area for bird watching. Polly Joke beach has no catering facilities, but is dog friendly all year round.

Cubert Common houses a massive barrow on the far south edge of the Common, which is now owned by the National Trust. The barrow is vast, with a great view to the sea, so may have been built for an important local burial. This walk was done in early spring.

Distance	Shorter walk is 3 miles; longer route is 4 miles long
Time	Shorter walk is 1½ hours; longer walk is 2 hours
Terrain	Easy going, some steep hills
Parking and public toilets	National Trust car parks at Polly Joke and Crantock Beach. Public toilets at Crantock Beach
Refreshments	The Bowgie Inn, West Pentire, or The Albion Inn at Crantock Village. Crantock village also has a shop and teashop
Map	OS Explorer 104 Redruth and St Agnes

The Walk

At Chiverton Cross roundabout, take the A3075 to Newquay and continue past Goonhavern until reaching a small left hand turn signposted to West Pentire and Crantock. After Crantock village, follow the signs to West Pentire, and at the end of the road Crantock Bay Hotel is on the right and

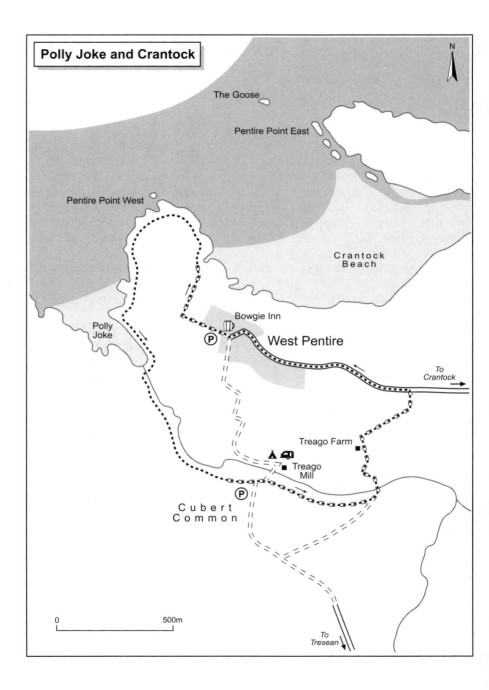

Polly Joke and Crantock

N

The Goose

Pentire Point East

Pentire Point West

Crantock
Beach

Bowgie Inn

Polly
Joke

West Pentire

To
Crantock

Treago Farm

Treago
Mill

Cubert
Common

0   500m

To
Tresean

West Pentire cliffs

the Bowgie (Cornish for cow shed) pub straight ahead. A public car park is just round the corner on the left.

From this car park, return to the main road, bear round to the right, and go through a gate leading to West Pentire Head. Tamarisk hedges lie to the right, over which the sun glistens on the River Gannel estuary and the sand dunes of Crantock Beach. Continue along this path until reaching the grassy headland of West Pentire that at various times of the year is dotted with cowslips and poppies.

Walking out over the headland, note the feral rock pigeons that swoop and dive under the cliffs. Follow the coastal path round to the left, looking out on an azure sea covered in foam. Head downhill, past stunted tamarisk trees that are windblown and sparse and suddenly Polly Joke comes into view: like stumbling across a cove in paradise, it is so perfect, so unspoilt.

Continue along the narrow footpath which leads to a wooden kissing gate and onto the beach. If the tide is out, there is a wide expanse of pure

Polly Joke beach

golden sand, dotted with secret caves of swirly slate. These rocks were apparently formed during the Devonian period, about 350 million years ago, and quartz veins can be seen running through them.

A wide stream bisects the beach, so it is usually best to take the right hand fork though sand dunes, and make a detour along the sand, shells crunching underfoot. This beach is dog friendly all year round, and popular with families, despite or perhaps because of the fact that there is no café nearby. Swimmers and surfers also love this beach, and frequently bob in the waves like sleek seals, while sheep graze on Kelsey Head opposite, silhouetted against a deep blue sky.

Returning to the path, cross the footbridge and take the right hand path through sand dunes and up through several gates. The path is narrow and well worn, covered in years of sand, and passes by a large campsite on the left before emerging into a small field that is a National Trust car park. The elegant house of Treago Mill lies to the left, while Cubert Common climbs up on the right, the sunshine casting swooping shadows over the marram grass. If you stop and listen on a winter's day, the only sounds are the rustling stream and skylarks tweeting above.

Leave the car park via another five barred gate which runs over a tiny stream, and follow a rough track through Cubert Common but look out for Bronze Age barrows. According to legend, if any of these are disturbed, disaster will come upon Cubert village. As they are all intact, it seems that legend is a good deterrent.

The rough track winds its way beside the campsite and veers round to the left, to Higher Moor house on the left and a fishing pond on the right, where fisherman enjoy the tranquility, surrounded by a gaggle of Barnacle geese. Go through yet another gate and climb the steep narrow hill, with Treago Farm campsite sprawled on the right – chalets and tents are available here – and converted barns that now house a shop and bar on the left. At the top of the hill is a T-junction – turn left here and return along the road that leads back to the Bowgie pub and car park.

For a longer walk, drive into Crantock village square and keep left, taking the road signposted 'To the Beach' and park in the National Trust car park next to the beach. Take the path behind the public toilets, through the sand dunes, keeping to the left at the top of the hill. This path skirts the edge of fields and descends to a footbridge, then uphill, round to the left in front of the Crantock Bay Hotel. Keeping to the seawards path, this continues on to West Pentire Point which leads down to Polly Joke. From there take the inland path as in the shorter walk and follow directions as far as the top of the hill after Treago Farm campsite. Turn right and then first left into Crantock village, and follow signs back to the beach and car park.

Other local places of interest

Bronze Age barrows on Cubert Common.

Crantock has a holy well in the centre of the village and another, dedicated to St Ambrose, halfway down the road to the beach.

5. Chapel Porth, St Agnes

A spectacular coastal walk round some of Cornwall's mining areas including Wheal Coates mine engine – the most photographed mine engine in Cornwall

Chapel Porth is approximately two miles from St Agnes; a relatively small beach which at low tide boasts miles of white sand which stretch to the next beach at Porthtowan. Alternatively, the South West coast path extends along the cliff top in either direction. A lifeguard service operates daily from May to September. Areas of historical interest include the Bronze Age barrow on St Agnes beacon, Wheal Coates mine buildings, and the remains of Cameron training Camp. Chapel Porth is situated on the North Cornwall coast just South of St Agnes. The area here is owned and managed by the National Trust, and there is a small car park and café. The beach is a small sandy cove which at low tide extends to a wide strip beyond the cliffs. This walk was done in late summer.

Distance	3 miles
Time	Approximately 2 hours
Terrain	Steep in places and many rocky paths
Refreshments	Café and toilets at Chapel Porth beach
Map	OS Explorer 104 Redruth and St Agnes

The Walk

Take the A30 Redruth-Bodmin road, and turn left onto the B3277 for St Agnes, following the signs to Chapel Porth. The road leading down to the beach is steep and narrow with few passing places, and at the bottom of the hill park in the National Trust car park, which also has a café serving a wide range of delicious goodies, and public toilets. The words 'Chapel Porth' embedded in white stones on the opposite cliff confirms the destination.

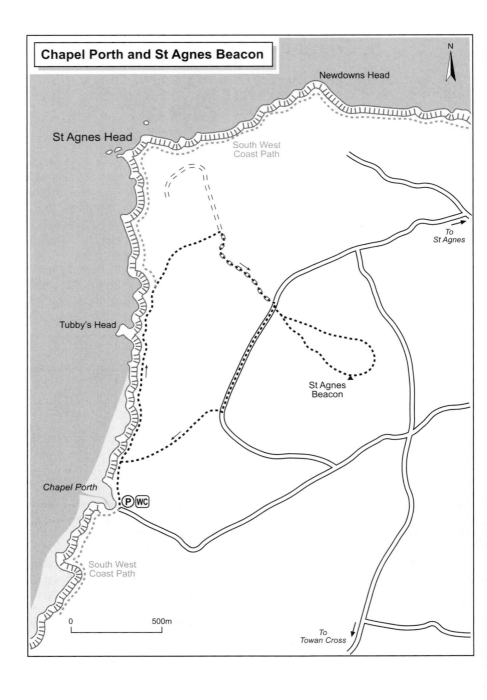

Chapel Porth and St Agnes Beacon

With the sea on the left, take a steep rocky path up the cliff and climb up to a rocky outcrop with awe inspiring views: from here can be seen the beaches of Portreath and Porthtowan, on the skyline a silhouette of the old arsenic works at Poldice, and Nancekuke, the chemical defence site at Portreath. Follow the coastal path until reaching the engine house for the Towanroath shaft of Wheal Coates mine which has been carefully restored by the National Trust. This is the most photographed mine engine in Cornwall and provided the frontispiece for Daphne du Maurier's book *Vanishing Cornwall*.

Turn right here and climb up a rocky path with stones of autumn colours – deep yellow, red, black and strains of blue. This path leads to the remains of the Wheal Coates mine buildings where tin and copper were mined between 1820 and 1914 – the copper can still be seen as blue streaks in some of the surrounding stone.

Turn left and head away from the coast, towards a wider path over the headland. The terrain flattens here, with gorse and heather on each side,

Towanroath engine house of Wheal Coates

Hang glider by Wheal Coates

and fields on the right leading up to St Agnes Beacon which have proved popular with those looking for a different venue for a wedding party.

A diagonal path to the right leads to a tarmac road and a huge lump of pockmarked porous granite, threaded with veins of Cassiterite, and spots of Haematite: proof of the rich mining heritage of this area. Overhead gliders can often be seen soaring by from Perranporth Airfield.

A few hundred yards further on is a sentry box that marks the site of the Cameron training camp for the 100th Light Anti-Aircraft battery. From 1943-44 it housed American army units prior to embarkation to France. After the war, the bungalows provided accommodation for local families until more council houses were built.

The tarmac road leads to a T-junction and opposite, a path that led up to St Agnes Beacon. Several million years ago, this beacon was an island and mining evidence shows that there was a pebbly beach at about the same height as today's ground level. Now the old sea floor shoreline is covered in thick layers of china clay which is extracted in the Newdown Sand and Clay Pits, further along the road.

St Agnes Beacon is a granite outcrop with Bronze Age barrows on the summit, where bonfires are lit on Midsummer Eve and other special occasions. On a clear day it is possible to see 30 church spires or towers, and from the highest point of 192 metres (628 feet) the views are incredible – westwards is St Ives, and Trevose Head near Padstow in the north. It is sometimes possible to make out the 'Cornish Alps' – the china clay tips in the distance to the south and, nearer, the granite outcrop of Carn Brea.

Return to the road, turn left past Bungay Yard, home of a farrier and blacksmith, and turn right, onto moorland, back towards Chapel Porth. The path back to Wheal Coates is steep and flanked by grey hawthorn thickets, dense and prickly, and finally the path returns to Chapel Porth beach.

Note
Dogs are banned from this beach from Easter Sunday until 30th September inclusive .

6. The Hall Walk
A creekside walk from Polruan to Bodinnick-By-Fowey

Fowey is situated on the South Coast of Cornwall and is an Area of Outstanding Natural Beauty. It lies at the end of the Saints' Way and has a foot ferry over to the village of Polruan opposite, and a vehicle ferry over to Bodinnick.

From 1300, when the town of Fowey was established, the natural harbour encouraged trade to develop with Europe and local ship owners often hired vessels to the king to support various wars, though piracy was prevalent at this time. In the 14th century two blockhouses were built on either side of the harbour entrance, but despite these Fowey was attacked by French forces in 1457. A small castle was built on St Catherine's Point in 1540 which enabled soldiers to beat off an attack by the Dutch in 1667.

The Mohun family of Hall, once the most important manor in the area, created this walk in 1585 as an early example of a private ornamental promenade, with terraced gardens which zig-zagged down the hillside to the river. Sir Arthur Quiller-Couch, famous writer and scholar, leased part

Distance	4 miles
Time	2 hours but allow extra for ferries
Terrain	Steep in parts; muddy in places
Polruan ferry	Foot passengers/cyclists only £1.20 single fare, dogs 30p (prices at time of travelling) Phone: 01726 832626
Bodinnick ferry	Pedestrians/vehicles, no coaches £1.20 single fare for passengers. Phone: 01726 870232
Refreshments	The Old Ferry Inn, Bodinnick-by-Fowey. 01726 870237 www.oldferryinn.co.uk Pinky Murphy's café, 19 North Street, Fowey. 01726 832512 www.pinkymurphys.com Numerous pubs in Polruan and Fowey
Map	OS Explorer 107 St Austell and Liskeard

of the gardens in the early 1900s. The walk was given to the National Trust as a joint memorial to those who died in the Second World War, and to Sir Arthur Quiller-Couch. This walk was done in March.

The Walk

Leaving St Austell, take the A390 then turn right onto the A3082 which leads through Par. Arriving in Fowey, park in the main car park at the top of the town and walk down to Town Quay to catch the ferry over to Polruan. (In summer the ferry leaves from Whitehouse Quay, along the Esplanade.) The ferry only takes a few minutes to Polruan Quay – but check the last ferry times back just to be sure.

Past The Lugger pub turn right up the hill then left into East Street which climbs above Tom's Boatyard to find a wooden sign indicating 'Hall Walk' to the right. Follow the steep steps up, turn left past another sign and onto a woodland path. Looking across to Fowey, yellow moorings were scattered across the harbour like hundreds and thousands, and there were wonderful views over shingled roofs and the turreted castle of Place Manor. It is clear to see why Mabel Lucie Attwell painted her famous fairies and elves here.

Given past winters, a friend had suggested a mud rating, with 10 being the highest. Along here was a 6, but there were plenty of wooden seats thoughtfully provided for weary legs. Continue past exotic ferns and catkins and take a detour down to the left which leads down more steps and young holly and hazel trees. These woods provide a safe refuge for dormice, which climb the trees and shrubs when they come out of hibernation. Continue down through oak trees until reaching a beautiful engraving about five foot tall, showing the effect of the coppicing on butterflies, animals and woodworkers.

Pont Pill Farm buildings

Here turn right, parallel to the river, with views over the estuary, Pont Pill, on the left. Leo Walmsley lived in a disused army hut here in the 1930s and 1950s and wrote about it in *Love in the Sun* and *Paradise Creek*.

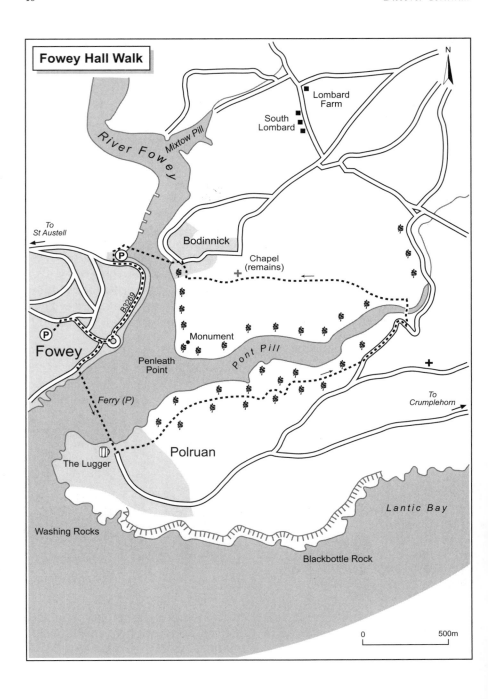

Climbing uphill, return to the main path and follow signs to Pont through the sun dappled woods where a stream tumbles in the distance. The next section can be very sticky (mud rating 4, rising to 6), and pass a sign to Lanteglos Church, where Daphne du Maurier married in 1932 and featured as Lanoc Church in her first novel *The Loving Spirit*. Following the signs to Pont, look down through dense woods on the opposite river bank, grey and silver tipped, like a setting for a Tim Burton film. Decayed tree roots smothered in black seaweed litter the river basin, like some eerie swamp, and a silent heron waits, still as a statue.

Heading downhill through mud rating 8, then a carpet of snowdrops and wild garlic leaves, cross a fast running stream and reach Pont Creek. Kenneth Grahame was one of many writers who lived in this unspoilt haven of peaceful tranquility. Pont, or pons means bridge in Cornish, and many years ago this hamlet was an important river quay when sailing barges came up river to unload coal, fertiliser, limestone, timber, roadstone and fresh produce from the farms in this area of Lanteglos. Pont Pill Farmhouse dates from the 18th century and was The Ship pub at one time.

Overlooking Fowey

Cross the modernised footbridge at Pont (which dates back to 1478), veer to the right, then take a sharp left to the other side of the creek. Here in spring are clumps of dark violets, a shy periwinkle and primroses nestling next to tufts of wild chives. Climb to the top of a steep hill, and rest – don't undertake this walk unless you're reasonably fit or, like me, had cake for lunch.

At the top of the hill, the tip of Lanteglos church peeped through the trees while far below the river turned from a muddy sludge to the most incredible aquamarine. The spring lichen was a pale feathery green, interspersed with catkins, and from an oak tree came the piercingly sweet song of a coal tit. It is so high here I was almost at eye level with a kestrel, floating on thermals until it was chased away by irate seagulls.

Passing through a kissing gate, go over a stile past a massive fallen tree like a huge dinosaur. Turn the corner for your first glimpse of the red and white striped tower of Gribbin Head in the shimmering distance. Nearer are the remains of St Catherine's Castle at Readymoney, and Polruan with cottages clustered on the hill like a drawing from a children's book.

Soon you approach Penleath Point, which is marked by a memorial to Sir Arthur Quiller-Couch, or 'Q', who wrote of Fowey: '...the tides of which time has since woven so close into the pulse of my own life that memory cannot now separate the rhythms'.

Rounding the corner, walk past a war memorial and look back for one last glimpse at Fowey before descending to the hamlet of Bodinnick. The cream fronted house at the bottom of the hill was Daphne du Maurier's first Cornish home – the Swiss Cottage – which she renamed Ferryside.

Board the Bodinnick ferry and head back over the river to Caffa Mill car park. Turn left along Passage Street, back into town. Here you will find Pinky Murphy's café, which is well worth a visit.

7. Par to Polkerris

Start off on the beach at Par, discover the magical village of Polkerris and return via the coastal footpath

Polkerris (meaning 'fortified pool' in Cornish) is on the east side of St Austell Bay, two miles west of Fowey and three miles east of St Austell. From the 17th century, fishing was the mainstay of the village's economy until the fish stocks collapsed due to overfishing. Tourism became significant from the 1950s and today the village has restaurants, water sports and some accommodation. In 1859 the RNLI built a lifeboat station here helped by donations of cash, land and building materials from William Rashleigh. The station was closed in 1922 when a lifeboat was stationed at Fowey for the first time. This walk was done on a glorious day in September.

Distance	2½ miles
Time	Just under 1½ hours
Terrain	A few steep hills, paths can be very muddy after rain. Varied views, landscape and wildlife
Car park	Par Beach £2.10 all day at time of writing. Car park also at Polkerris
Public toilets	At Polkerris
Refreshments	Ship Inn at Par, Rashleigh Arms and Sam's café, Polkerris café at Polkerris
Map	OS Explorer 107 St Austell and Liskeard

The Walk

From Fowey, take the main St Austell road (A3082), turning left just before the railway bridge at the bottom of Polmear Hill, past the Ship pub. Continue along this road for several hundred yards and park in the car park on the left, near Par Beach, which is free in winter.

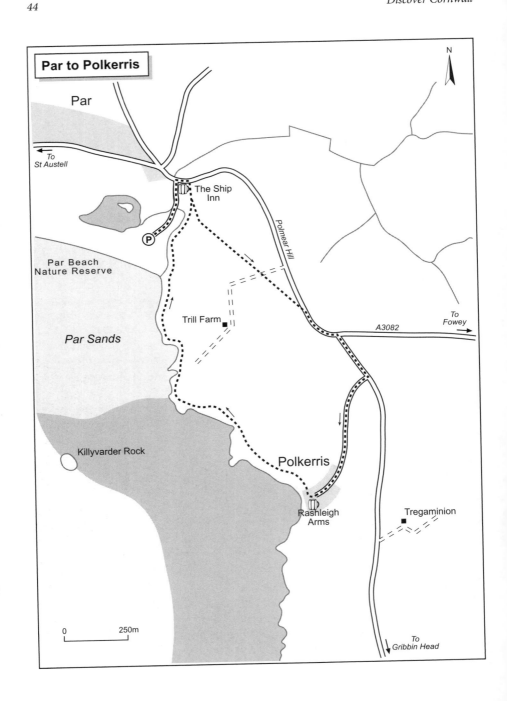

Walk back towards the Ship pub with a row of almshouses next door: these were built in 1650 by the Rashleigh family and converted into modern houses in 1977/8. By Chapel Cottage follow the Saints Way sign and a yellow waymark leading uphill to a very steep path, populated by holly trees and often festooned with particularly vicious nettles. At the top of this hill is a large field at the time inhabited by several horses belonging to the nearby riding school.

Walk across the field where a faint path can be seen through the grass heading towards the trees on the skyline. Looking down over the huge Par Beach is a fabulous sight: St Austell Bay stretches out in the distance, while the china clay chimneys smoulder around Par Harbour, and a huge pool can be seen, next door to a caravan park.

Turn right here, parallel to the hedge, heading inland until reaching another stile on the right, with a rotted waymark sign lying on the ground. Walk diagonally left until reaching a double wooden and granite stile in the corner of the field which leads to the busy road heading down Polmear Hill.

Rashleigh Arms, Polkerris

St Austell Bay

Cross the road to reach the pavement on the opposite side and head uphill. Past the sign to Trill Horse Trail take the first turning on the right, signposted to 'Polkerris Beach and Menabilly', past a lone letterbox. Turn right again down to Polkerris, where the hill leading downwards is extremely narrow and steep, with high banks on either side.

Walk past a cottage draped in Virginia Creeper and continue down to Polkerris which consists of several pretty whitewashed cottages with beautiful fuchsias growing in abundance outside. Public toilets are off on the left. Until the end of the 19th century, Polkerris had one of the largest fish cellars in Cornwall, which still dominate the beach, and a huge fleet of seine boats.

At the bottom of the hill is the Rashleigh Arms, which was orginally in what is now the car park: the present pub building was once a boat shed. The pub was the setting for the 1972 film *Doomwatch*, which was a spin-off of the BBC TV series. The granite wall of the harbour curves like a strong protective arm, and you can see several canons tipped up to act as bollards. This pier was built by the Rashleigh family around 1730 and what is now Sam's café was the old lifeboat house. Head uphill in front of a couple of cottages with gardens on either side, planted on an almost sheer cliff face.

A thoughtfully placed bench has been placed at the top of this hill and provides a good place to sit and have a drink of water and admire the view down onto Polkerris beach, up through the neighbouring woods and out over St Austell Bay.

Rested, continue back along the coastal path where on a good day the sun shines silver on the water far out to sea and the tip of Gribben Head is just visible over the tops of the far hills. The path winds round back to Par beach, past fields of sheep, and back to the car park.

Note
Dogs are allowed on Par Beach all year round.

8. Malpas
A creekside walk not far from Truro

The love story of Tristan and Iseult tells how Iseult crossed the Truro River at La Mal Pas (pronounced Mopus) to meet her lover as she travelled from Moresk to Kea. Malpas derives from the French 'mal pas' meaning 'bad passage', because of the dangerous waterways here, where whirlpools and tidal waves have been reported.

Jenny Davies, also known as Jenny Mopus, ran the ferry until she died aged 82, in 1832. Jenny stated that her worst passengers were "wemmin and pigs", and her portrait hangs at Tregothnan house, although the house and estate are private and not open to the public.

There was once an important oyster bed here at Malpas, and many ships carried coal and other commodities along this stretch of the river during the industrial heyday of the 19th century. The huge ships carrying timber from Norway anchored here for their cargo to be unloaded onto rafts to be taken up the shallower stretch of the river to Truro and the mines beyond. This walk was done on a wet day in January.

Distance	**Approximately 4 miles**
Time	**2¼ hours**
Terrain	**A few steep hills, can be very muddy**
Refreshments	**The Heron Inn, Trenhaile Terrace, Malpas TR1 1SL** **Tel: 01872 272773; info@heronInn.co.uk**
Map	**OS Explorer 105 Falmouth and Mevagissey**

The Walk

Arriving at the Trafalgar roundabout in Truro, turn left at the signpost to Malpas, and continue until reaching the tiny village of Malpas, and park in the road. This village is built at the conjunction of three rivers – the Tresillian River, the arm of Truro River leading to the city and the Truro River as it flows towards the Fal and Carrick Roads.

St Clement Church

Follow a yellow waymark sign on the right saying 'St Clement' which leads along a private road, round the back of some houses and into a very muddy path. Pass through a wooden kissing gate and into dense woods where tendrils of Old Man's Beard tumble into a fast flowing stream, and emerald green moss grows up the tree trunks.

Over a makeshift bridge, follow a waymark sign to 'St Clement – Denas Road' to the right is an alternative route by the creek. At the top of this hill, pass through a metal kissing gate and into another field. The next waymark sign guides you through another kissing gate, and turn right before emerging into another field. Below the church of St Clement (1326) nestles in a valley where gentle sunlight kisses the tops of the trees.

Pass through another kissing gate into St Clement and turn right, past Elm Cottage where old teacups hang from hooks around the outside. Continue downhill past beautiful old cottages, down to the river. The woodland on the far bank is part of the Tregothnan Estate, home to the Boscawen family since 1335. This working estate is internationally known for producing the only tea grown in England, but the diversity of lands

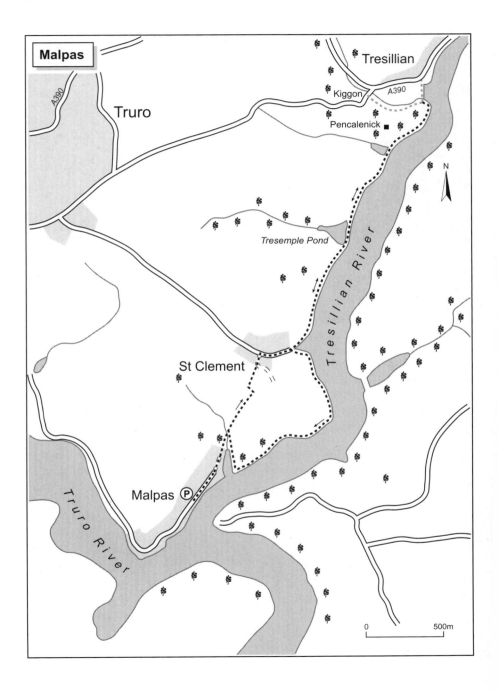

also allows the production of sustainable coppiced charcoal, Manuka honey and Kea plum jam as well as seasonal British flowers for a range of hand-tied bouquets. (See **http://tregothnan.co.uk**)

Tresemple Pond is passed on the left: this is a popular place for bird watching as birds such as oyster-catchers, curlew and redshanks feed on the exposed mudflats. Herons and egrets are common visitors to the area too, and at high tide you may catch a glimpse of a kingfisher.

Continue until reaching a footbridge on the right which leads through a marshy area to Tresillian; it is possible to turn left and walk back to Truro via the road, but for this walk, retrace your steps until arriving back in the hamlet of St Clement and turn left along Denas Road, which leads back along the shore line. This path passes into woods of dense pines then opens out over various stiles into fields, more woodland, until finally Malpas comes into sight. Continue to the junction in the woods where you started off, back round the houses and along the road back to the car.

Tresillian river

9. Coombe and Cowlands Creeks

A gentle walk round Coombe and Cowlands Creeks, home of the famous Kea Plums

This is a popular walk with locals because of its wonderful views of the picturesque creek at Coombe and the River Fal. When walking through the surrounding woods, cargo carriers are often seen moored up in the deep waters here, waiting for their next voyage. In the past the main industries of this area were plum growing, oyster dredging, resin for the leather industry (obtained from 'barking' oak trees), and the production of mineral ore. Now there is no industry: even the houses offering cream teas have become a thing of the past.

Kea plums are exclusive to this area and used to provide an important income to the villagers, though the season is only two weeks between late August and early September. Kea plums are the size of damsons and too sharp to eat fresh, but make the most fabulous jam. More recently, Cornish producers have diversified into making ice cream, cider, wine and even chocolates from these little fruits. The name is taken from the Irish Saint Kea who, after floating from Ireland on a granite boulder, is supposed to have landed where old Kea church stood. This walk was done in early spring.

Distance	3 miles
Time	Approximately 1½ hours
Terrain	A few steep hills but otherwise easy going though can be muddy in parts
Refreshments	Punchbowl and Ladle Inn at Penelewey, near Feock
Map	OS Explorer 105 Falmouth and Mevagissey

The Walk

Take the A39 Truro to Falmouth road, and turn off at Playing Place for the King Harry Ferry turning. This passes through Penelewey and just past

Coombe Creek

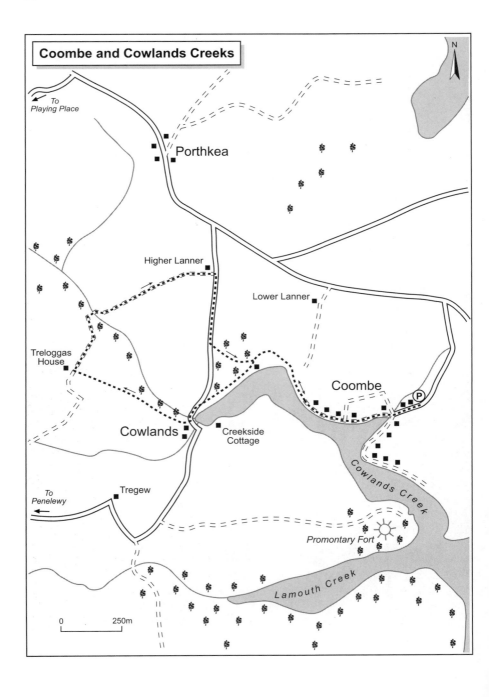

Coombe and Cowlands Creeks

To Playing Place

Porthkea

Higher Lanner

Lower Lanner

Treloggas House

Coombe

P

Cowlands

Creekside Cottage

To Penelewy

Tregew

Cowlands Creek

Promontary Fort

Lamouth Creek

0   250m

the Punchbowl and Ladle pub is a turning signposted to 'Coombe'. Continue along this road, through Porthkea and turn sharp right down to Coombe.

After the second cattle grid, park in a layby on the left, then walk down to the creek. When the tide is out the thick mud banks here lie like sleeping elephants, and gulls shriek while mallards bathe and quack. Walking past several old boat hulls, there are two wooden benches, positioned to give a perfect view up the creek.

The path grows narrower here and leads past a settlement on the opposite bank with a run down quay, several moored vessels like ghost ships, and a home made red flag. The inhabitant is a recluse who does not welcome visitors, so please respect his privacy.

Overhanging oak trees with roots rubbed bare by years of erosion accompany the rest of the path until you reach the foreshore. Turn right here following a yellow arrow marking the footpath (a 'waymark') up to a cottage that has recently been refurbished. There used to be a ramshackle

Looking towards Cowlands

stall of nick nacks here, constructed on railway sleepers, perched over a running stream. Locals always stopped to browse the goods on offer, which never failed to delight.

Follow the waymarks through a steep field on the left until reaching a wooden stile that leads into a wood that is frequently extremely muddy. Further on is a whitewashed cob cottage and a public footpath sign pointing to the right towards Cowlands. Follow yet another muddy track through woods with holly trees on either side until reaching the road. Turn left here, down the hill to Cowlands Creek, home to one of Britain's best known potters, Mary Rich.

Standing at the head of the creek, on the left is an orchard of Kea plums, some of which grow on the foreshore where they are sheltered from the south-westerly winds. On the other side of Cowlands Creek is a huge fake thatched Georgian house that has been the cause of endless controversy in the area. A public footpath sign leads around the back of the house,

Curlew

into woods with a fast flowing stream. Some of the trees are covered in a brilliant emerald green lichen, and further on is an old quarry where the stone is covered in dense ferns and ivy that tumbles to the ground like dreadlocks.

This path leads into a steep field. Climb up here and at the end is a wooden stile with steep steps either side. Take the right hand turning, where a red arrow leads down a steep tarmac path, like a drover's lane with steep walls covered in ferns. This path dipped down then up past a farm; turn right at the junction of a muddy lane and look through a gate towards several huge ships laid up the Truro river – an uncomfortable reminder of the ongoing recession.

Continue down the lane until reaching a public footpath sign on the left, leading back into woods.

The steep path winds down through the trees and down a steep gully before arriving back at the foreshore, by the whitewashed cottage in the woods, and continue back the way you have come.

In spring notice clusters of snowdrops perched above a slate wall; a single primrose, and violet periwinkles, while further down the creek can often be seen egrets, silhouetted against the mudbanks and incoming tide.

Local place of interest
Mary Rich, Potter **www.maryrich.co.uk**

10. Bissoe Walk

A walk along part of the Bissoe cycle trail, through old mining country

This walk gives a real insight into one of the mining areas of Cornwall, undisturbed and ancient, where the air is heavy with history. The old Mineral Tramways from Devoran to Portreath is an interesting ride for the average cyclist – the route follows what were working rail tracks that carried minerals (tin, copper etc) to the ancient quays at Devoran or the harbour at Portreath. Mount Wellington Mine was once part of Wheal Jane and one of the last 3 working mines in Cornwall during the 1980s. This walk was done in late summer.

Distance	3¼ miles
Time	1½ - 2 hours
Terrain	Moderate but can be muddy in places so boots are advised
Refreshments	Available at Bissoe Tramways Cycle Hire. Over 100 Bikes Open all year. Old Conns Works, Bissoe Truro, TR4 8QZ Tel: 01872 870341
Map	OS Explorer 104 Redruth and St Agnes

The Walk

Take the A39 from Falmouth to Truro, and at the Devoran roundabout at the bottom of the hill take the turning marked Bissoe. This leads under a viaduct, past Bissoe Cycle Hire – take the first small turning on the right opposite a garage. Several hundred yards later is a granite post marked 'Wheal Andrew' and a little further down the road, park in a large layby on the right.

From here walk 100 yards on and take a steep rocky lane on the left by a granite sign to 'Twelveheads'. This area is known as Wheal Fortune and the land here was once the most expensive in Cornwall. From 1819 Wheal Fortune formed the easternmost part of the Great Gwennap Consolidated Mines, which was once the largest copper mine in the world. Although it worked for tin at an early period, it was as a copper mine that it became important. But cheaper ores were being mined abroad, and in England the price of copper fell from £115 to £80 a ton. In 1870 Wheal Fortune was abandoned and across Cornwall many miners emigrated to work in Australia and North America. There is little sign of wealth now: only a few scattered houses in amongst granite, bracken and heather.

Bissoe cycle trail

Follow this path up the hill, then down past Arley Cottage on the right, cross over a road and continue over, passing clumps of puffball mushrooms, like dun coloured pincushions. Continue up the hill, past Fernysplatt Bal, disused mine dumps and mine workings. At the top of the hill take a left fork, past White Cottage on the left, and follow this rocky path downhill through thick mud churned up by cycle tracks. Look out over high hedges onto fields of lush tall grass, and at the end of the footpath turn right into a small road which leads to the tiny hamlet of Coombe Hill. Clifford House is on the left and an orchard studded with bright red apples.

Further down the road descend into a dense wooded valley where the river rumbles noisily below. At the bottom of this road turn right and first left at a public footpath sign, partly obscured by an oak tree laden with green acorns, and enter another small hamlet. Here are stables on the right, and a rusty dustbin perched incongruously on the bank of a fast running stream. Further on turn left to follow another public footpath sign, over a bridge where the stream swells to a river, then plunges into a

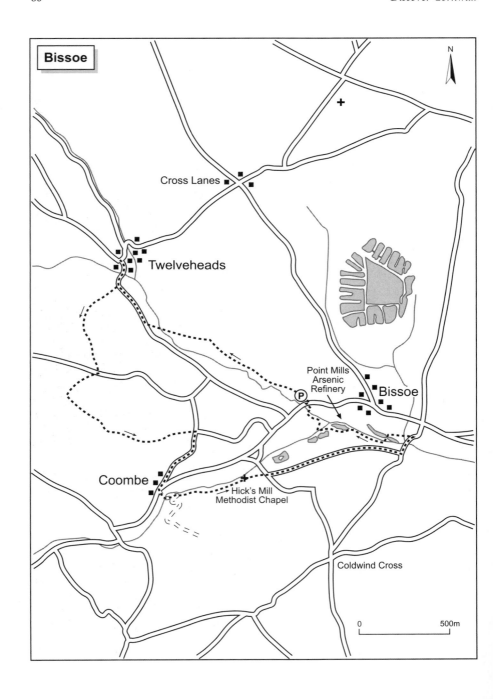

Bissoe

N

Cross Lanes

Twelveheads

Point Mills
Arsenic
Refinery

Bissoe

Coombe

Hick's Mill
Methodist Chapel

Coldwind Cross

0   500m

whirling eddy. Here the slender trees are throttled with thick veins of ivy, and the path is often heavy with mud.

The path suddenly opens out into a tarmac area – pass Calico Cottage before arriving at Hicks Mill Methodist Church, built in 1821, though the deeds go back to 1667 and there was once a corn mill on this site. Continue past this well maintained building and walk through the car park out onto a road and turn immediately right then left, along a quiet road past Mount Pleasant Farm on the right. This leads to another crossroads – turn left. Over the granite bridge turn left onto the official cycle trail from Devoran to Portreath; this is a smoother track, popular with cyclists of all ages and sizes.

Continue over another wooden bridge, and notice red water flowing in the stream below: this was from heavy metals that leaked into the water when Wheal Jane mine flooded in 1991, leaching toxic mine waste that travelled as far as Restronguet Creek. The ground opens up here into flat moorland with gorse and purple heather. Looking up see cement works that look eerily like a James Bond set. Mount Wellington looks down from the left, and all around is Bissoe Valley Nature Reserve owned by the Wildlife Trust. A restoration programme set up in 1986 has ensured that there is newly planted woodland, ponds and regenerating heathland in this area and evidence of this can be seen: a pond with huge lemon coloured waterlillies in amongst the reeds, dragonflies and emerald damsel flies.

Further on is what looks like a solitary mine engine but is in fact what was left of the Point Mills Arsenic Refinery, that produced arsenic famous for its high quality throughout Europe. A plaque

An old millrace near Coombe Lane

advises that the refinery operated for 100 years ending with the outbreak of the Second World War.

Continue towards the road, turn left and immediately right to Bissoe Cycle Hire where there is a café that serves a variety of drinks and cakes, as well as supplying bicycles. Leaving the cycle hire behind, head onto a narrow and muddy path. Soon the path forks and meets up with another bridlepath. This is smoother which makes walking easier and a little further on is the official cycle trail with a mine waste dump towering on the right.

Finally, arrive back at Wheal Andrew, turn right and walk along the road to the layby where the car is parked.

11. Carn Marth

A walk taking in one of the highest hills in West Cornwall, home to an open air theatre built in a quarry

Carn Marth lies a couple of miles southeast of Redruth and is 771 feet high. One of several ancient hills that runs down Cornwall's spine, it provided perfect sites for beacons to warn of impending attack, mark victories and celebrations of all sorts. There is also an open air theatre and the view from the top of Carn Marth is one of the few places in Cornwall from where both coasts can be seen. On a clear day, Carn Marth can be seen from Bodmin Moor – over 30 miles away.

The top of Carn Marth is covered in heath, bracken, gorse and a wonderful mix of wild flowers, as well as being a good birdwatching place. Swallows, cuckoos and warblers populate the flooded quarries, while peregrines and buzzards can be seen soaring overhead. On the lower areas of Carn Marth are grazing fields surrounded by ancient Cornish hedges. This walk was done in late spring.

Distance	3 miles
Time	1½ hours
Terrain	Steep in parts
Refreshments	The Fox and Hounds, Comford. Lanner Garden Centre
Map	OS Explorer 104, Redruth and St Agnes

The Walk

From Falmouth take the A393 towards Redruth, going through Ponsanooth, then Lanner. Climbing the hill out of Lanner, take a turning on the right called 'Pennance Road' and continue along here until a traffic calming section with a notice saying 'Priority Over Oncoming Traffic'. Park in a layby just past this on the left and take the footpath leading uphill.

The path curves round to the left, past Carn Marth House and Carn Marth Barn and climbs higher, where the path grows sandy, looking down over

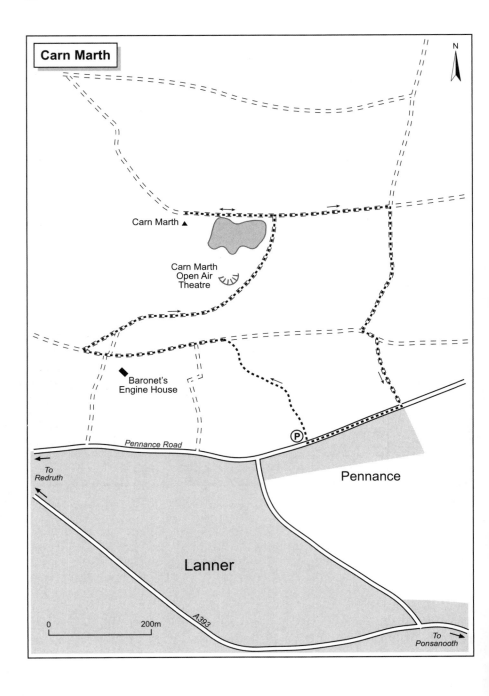

Carn Marth

N

Carn Marth ▲

Carn Marth
Open Air
Theatre

Baronet's
Engine House

Pennance Road

To
Redruth

Pennance

Lanner

A393

To
Ponsanooth

0   200m

sparse moorland to Lanner on the left. Walking between gnarled moorland hedges, windblown and sparse, the path leads to a beautifully restored mine engine house which is Baronet's Engine House, built in 1866, formerly known as Wheal Amelia and part of Pennance Consols Mixed Mine.

Past Rockfield Farm, turn sharp right uphill past another farm, at the time marked by a huge Camellia bush with blowsy pink flowers. The concrete path leads to a sandy track and soon some red gates on the left marking Carn Marth theatre.

In 1986, when plans were proposed to reopen a granite quarry on Carn Marth and remove 1.5 million tons of granite, there was fierce opposition. The Carn Marth Protection Group was founded and with the help and support of thousands of people, near and far, the hill was saved and a portion of the top was bought by the Carn Marth Trust.

It was then decided to convert the lower quarry into an open air theatre, forming terraces for a seating area, and installing electricity. The first

Carn Marth upper quarry

Baronet's Engine House

production of *The Three Musketeers*, by Cornwall Theatre Company, was a great success, and generated much needed funds. Enthusiastic audiences of over four hundred brought cushions, blankets and food and drink.

Since those early days the Theatre Quarry has seen productions and performances every year by groups including Shiva, Kneehigh, Miracle, Hammered Steel, Carharrack and St Day Silver Band and Doreen Fiol's influential Children's Theatre. It has also been used for wedding and birthday celebrations. The auditorium is an impressive sight, hewn out of vast cliffs of granite that tower over the grassy stage, while jackdaws circle above the grassy tiered seats.

Leaving the theatre, walk out to the left, pass another flooded quarry, and climb higher and higher, until the land levels out and a small obelisk is reached. From here is the most incredible view – looking east past St Agnes Beacon to Bodmin Moor, Rough Tor and Brown Willy (the highest hill in Cornwall at 1375ft) can be seen on a bright day. To the north is the Bristol Channel and to the south the English Channel. St Anthony's Light is at the entrance to Carrick Roads with Pendennis Castle and Falmouth opposite. Further west is the reservoir at Stithians, then Carnmenellis and Carn Brea, with views across the Great Flat Lode and its engine houses.

At the next waymarked junction, by a derelict house, turn right along a grassy track that leads into a rocky path going downhill. At the next junction, marked by oak apple trees on the right, turn sharp left which leads back to the original path and the layby where the car is parked.

Note
More information on the Carn Marth Trust and open air theatre is available at **www.carnmarth.org.uk**

12. Mylor Quay

From Mylor Quay along the creek to the Pandora Inn, returning via Mylor Bridge

The Pandora Inn was once a Passage House, renamed The Pandora in memory of the 'HMS Pandora', the naval ship sent to Tahiti to capture the mutineers of Captain Bligh's 'Bounty'. Unfortunately, the 'Pandora' struck a remote part of the Great Barrier Reef in 1791 and sank with the loss of many crew and mutineers. The captain, Captain Edwards, was court-martialled on his return to Cornwall where he is reputed to have bought this inn.

The Pandora has been a popular pub with locals and visitors for many a year, but in March 2011, 40 firefighters were called to tackle a fire at the 13th Century thatched pub and restaurant near Falmouth. The whole of the roof was found to be well alight and then collapsed into the first floor. Heavy smoke emanated from the building, which is formerly a farmhouse with sections dating back to the 1200s and part of the upstairs of the St

Pandora Inn

Austell Brewery pub later collapsed as a result of the fire. The historical and much loved pub has since been rebuilt and opened again in March 2012. This walk was done in October.

Distance	3 miles
Time	1½ -2 hours
Terrain	Easy going, though can be very muddy. The hill up from the Pandora is very steep
Refreshments	Pandora Inn www.pandorainn.com 01326 3726768 Lemon Arms, Mylor Bridge 01326 373666 Various shops in Mylor Bridge
Map	OS Explorer 105 Falmouth and Mevagissey

The Walk

From Falmouth, take the A39 Falmouth-Penryn road and at Commercial Road, Penryn, take the road signposted to Mylor and continue until the village of Mylor Bridge. At the first mini-roundabout go straight over, then take the first sharp turning on the right, just before a few shops, and drive down past the post office to park on Mill Quay.

Walk along the road with public footpath signs to 'Greatwood and Restronguet'; swans and ducks populate this creek, looking down their noses at the riff-raff until they reach their own pool a little further on. Just past a circular mirror on the right, take a public footpath sign parallel to the creek and, for boating enthusiasts, enjoy the selection of boats at Tregatreath boatyard opposite.

The path curves round to the left, by a concrete block wall, then cross a private road and take the footpath sign ahead on the right, through a squeaky gate which leads to a large field. There are often cattle here – and bulls have been known. Cross the field, at the end of which there is a kind of metal kissing gate which leads to the foreshore, where boats lie marooned on the beach and gulls scream overhead.

Turn sharp left along the path that follows the creek – this next bit can be extremely muddy and slippery. On the opposite side of the creek are the

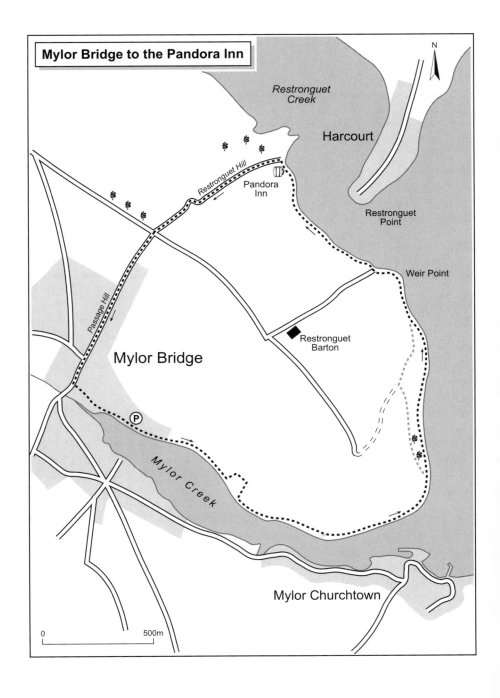

Mylor Bridge to the Pandora Inn

N

Restronguet Creek

Harcourt

Restronguet Hill

Pandora Inn

Restronguet Point

Weir Point

Passage Hill

Mylor Bridge

Restronguet Barton

P

Mylor Creek

Mylor Churchtown

0   500m

houses along Church Road – a selection of mostly retirement houses in varying shapes and sizes of grandeur. Walk past a ploughed field on the left, full of rich brown earth like chocolate fudge, and pass through another kissing gate. A winding path leads down to an overgrown quarry and on the shore, a couple of tired old boats lap up the sun in their last resting place. The path continues round to the right and another five barred gate into another field, then through that, to another little inlet with yet more decaying boats on the beach and a carefully positioned swing hanging from a tree over the beach.

Passing through another wooden kissing gate and another muddy quagmire, follow the path into another field, following a path diagonally uphill past a massive oak tree with branches trailing like a dowager's dress, through which the creek sparkled like diamonds. At the top of this hill is a dead tree, branches grasping their way skywards. The path now tumbles down the other side of the hill and in the winter, looking out to sea, are myriad moorings, in lurid shades of pink and green, like gobstoppers floating in the creek.

Passing through another wooden kissing gate, continue along a path strewn with acorns as far as Greatwood Quay, which provides good views over the waters of Carrick Roads, the Roseland Peninsula, and Mylor Harbour, where there used to be a naval dockyard. The remaining boats of the season were bobbing on the waves and the nearest of these belonged to BATS – Blind At Sea – who often sail on these waters.

Greatwood Quay is a listed building built in the 18th century, of vertically-set dry slatestone with dressed granite copings linked by iron staples. This beautifully built quay was a landing stage for Greatwood House, further along this path.

Continue along this path – in winter oyster fishing boats can be seen out in the Carrick Roads. Because oysters breed in the summer, fishing is restricted to October until April only. The Cornish have dredged for oysters in this area of the river Fal for over a century, and some of the boats, built at local boatyards, date back as far as 1860. Ancient laws were put in place to protect the natural ecology of the riverbeds and oyster stocks, stating that oystermen fishing in the Port of Truro Oyster Fishery are banned from using engines. Only sail power and hand-pulled dredges are permitted, although boats are allowed to motor out to the oyster beds.

This is the only oyster fishery in Europe, if not the world, where such traditional methods must be used, and watching a fisherman at work makes you realise what an art this work is.

This path continues uphill through the woods. At the end of this section of the path is a sign left to 'Restronguet Barton': this provides a shorter circular walk back to Mill Quay, but for this walk turn right which leads down to Greatwood House which was once a turreted mansion but is now converted to impressive looking flats with fabulous views out over the Carrick Roads. Further on is a row of small cottages, and the path continued past some old stables which were being renovated. There used to be several Shetland ponies that grazed here at an almost vertical angle.

Further on Gunnera leaves tower over the path, like giant plants from a nightmare, and the path leads to Weir Beach, another popular place for birds. There was once a solitary heron that would stand up the river, and a black swan that became quite famous. Often you will see egrets, curlews and the odd cormorant, perched on a buoy, drying its wings.

Tree above Mylor Creek

Leaving Weir Beach behind, continue along the path until you reach the Pandora Inn, parts of which date back to the 13th Century. Dogs are welcome here, and sitting outside in a sunny day, watching the goings on up and down Restronguet Creek is a relaxing pastime. Once refreshed, turn left up the hill which is extremely long, steep and narrow. At the top of this, continue over the crossroads and head down the hill, through the village of Mylor Bridge. Towards the bottom of the village, past the butcher (who sells very good pasties), is the turning to the left back to Mill Quay and starting point.

13. Mên-an-Tol

A moorland walk taking in stone circles, burial chambers and one of the Cornwall

The Penwith Peninsula in the far west of Cornwall is renowned as being of international importance in understanding ancient man's life. There are stone circles, burial chambers and standing stones in abundance, many of which date back to 2,000 years BC.

This walk takes in the famous Mên-an-Tol stones, Mên Scryfa; a commemoration to a sixth century chieftan, Nine Maidens stone circle, Lanyon Quoit and Ding Dong Mine engine house. Lanyon Quoit is thought to be a burial chamber of a long mound and was originally tall enough for a horseman to sit under. It collapsed in 1815 and reassembled in 1824 but to a smaller size than its original position.

It is thought that Mên-an-Tol is the remains of a chambered tomb, with the holed stone forming an entrance. The stones are said to provide healing, so naked children were passed through the hole three times and

Mên-an-Tol

Lanyon Quoit

drawn on the grass as a cure for tuberculosis and rickets. Adults would crawl through the hole as a cure for back complaints, but would need to go through nine times for it to work. Passing through the stone has also been used as a fertility aid, but there are many and varied stories attached to these stones. This walk was done in late September.

Distance	3 miles
Time	2 hours
Terrain	Easy going but some rough tracks and can be muddy in parts
Parking	Free parking opposite the old schoolhouse
Refreshments	Lanyon Farmhouse provide cream teas
Map	OS Explorer 102 Lands End, Penzance and St Ives

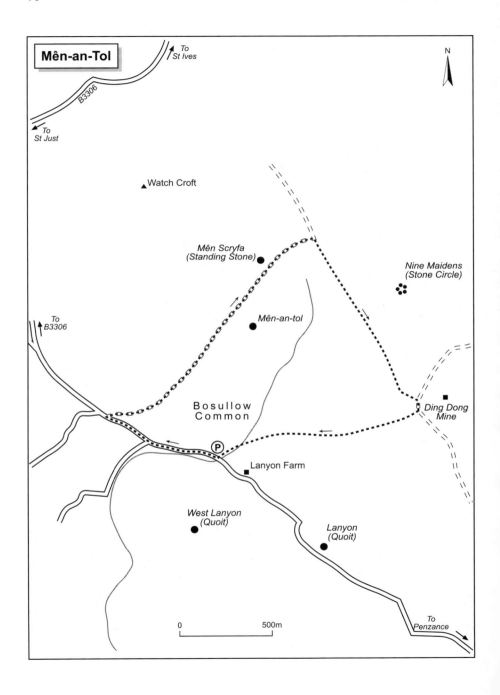

Mên-an-Tol

To St Ives

B3306

To St Just

N

Watch Croft

Mên Scryfa
(Standing Stone)

Nine Maidens
(Stone Circle)

To B3306

Mên-an-tol

Bosullow
Common

Ding Dong
Mine

P

Lanyon Farm

West Lanyon
(Quoit)

Lanyon
(Quoit)

0   500m

To
Penzance

The Walk

Leaving Penzance, take the Madron road and after about ten minutes pass Lanyon Quoit where you will find a small parking space on the right, opposite an old granite schoolhouse.

Head up a farm track and after 15 minutes turn right over a stile which leads to Mên-an-Tol. This megalithic monument is a wide, shallow stone one metre tall, carved into a circular shape and known as the Crick Stone or Devil's Eye. In the middle is a hole 45cm across and either side of this is a standing stone, about 1.2m tall.

Retrace your steps, returning to the original path and look out over Bosullow Common, illuminating Ding Dong Mine in the distance. Here is open moorland but hardly a tree in sight; mile after mile of scrubland interrupted by the occasional farm. A view that some find uplifting and magnificent but others find too harsh: there are none of the soft rolling hills of South East Cornwall here.

On the left is Mên Scryfa, a stone marking the grave of Rialobran, a sixth century chieftan warrior who was killed here around AD500. Continue up

Mên Scryfa

the very rough path and where it splits in front of a derelict building, take the right hand fork onto a track over moorland. This path climbs upwards, leading to Nine Maidens which are 11 spaced stones that do not in fact make a true circle. Boscawen Un Circle, as it's known in Cornish, was an ancient Druid meeting place and the location of the first Cornish Gorsedd. But the name refers to the phases of the lunar cycle rather than the number of stones. Legend has it that maidens dancing on the Sabbath were turned to stone, and the fiddler who supplied the music and followed their fate was the Blind Fiddler Menhir.

Follow a well worn path to the right through waist high gorse to Ding Dong Mine engine house, reputed to be one of the oldest mines in Cornwall. According to folklore Ding Dong worked 2000 years ago and was visited by Christ and Joseph of Arimathea, but the earliest mention of the mine was at the beginning of the 17th century. In 1714 three separate mines were operating: Good Fortune, Wheal Malkin and Hard Shafts Bounds, but Ding Dong did not become famous until the turn of the 18th century.

Coronation Farm

By the end of the 1850s the mine employed 206 men and boys, but was struggling to break even. Due to the continuing fall in the price of tin, the mine shut on 11 July 1877, following an unsuccessful attempt to sell it at auction. Since that time three other attempts have been made to reopen the mine; the first failed because of water problems and the other two through local opposition.

Standing at the engine house provides a fabulous view – in the distance stretches the Lizard, and below is Mounts Bay, with St Michael's Mount in the fairytale distance. There is a dizzying sense of height, and depth, and space here and it's still possible to catch a glimpse of Cornwall as it was many thousands of years ago.

Take a path below the engine house, across a stone stile and follow the path downhill for about 15 minutes. The narrow path twists and turns then take a right hand fork and reach a metal gate between stone walls which leads to the road. Turn right here and before long you will find Lanyon Farmhouse which provides a very good cream tea. From here it is a ten minute walk back to the car.

14. St Mawes

A varied circular walk taking in the village of St Mawes, the castle and National Trust headland

St Mawes used to be two villages – St Mawes and Bohella, separated by a small wall. Nowadays it is considered the capital of the Roseland by many and with good reason. The sailing facilities are excellent, there are many pubs, hotels and holiday accommodation, and the beaches are safe and good for swimming.

St Anthony lighthouse, which overlooks St Mawes, was built in 1834 to replace the old coal beacon and marks the entrance to the Carrick Roads which was created after the Ice Age when an ancient valley flooded and caused the sea level to rise dramatically. This turned into Falmouth harbour, the world's third natural largest harbour. The lighthouse keeps ships clear of the infamous Manacle Rocks and today it is automated and open to visitors.

St Mawes Castle is one of a chain of forts built by Henry VIII between 1539 and 1545 to counter an invasion threat from Catholic France and Spain. Together with Pendennis Castle on the other side of the Fal estuary, it guards the important anchorage of Carrick Roads. The castle is clover-leaf in shape, originally surrounded by octagonal outer defences and designed to mount heavy 'ship-sinking' guns. In 1646 it was attacked by Civil War Parliamentarian forces, and remained neglected until partial re-arming during the 19th and early 20th centuries. This walk was done in early summer.

Distance	1½ miles
Time	3 miles
Terrain	Easy going but a few very steep hills
King Harry Ferries	www.kingharryscornwall.co.uk/ferries/st_mawes_ferry
Refreshments	Victory Inn Phone 01326 270324
Map	OS Explorer 105, Falmouth and Mevagissey

View over to St Just

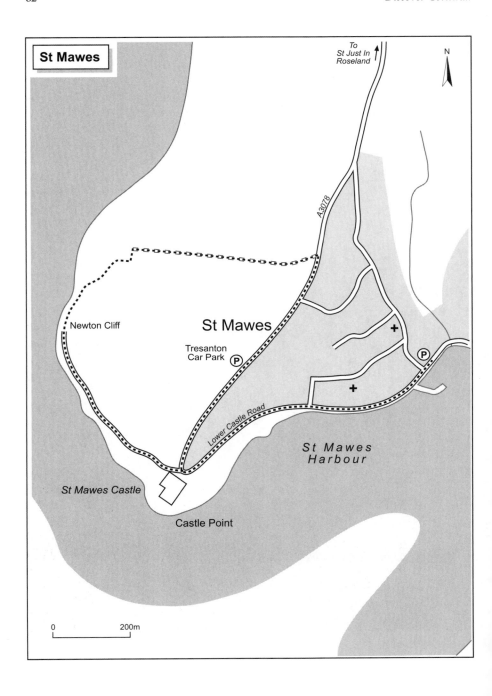

The Walk

To do this walk leaving the car behind, take the pedestrian ferry from Prince of Wales Pier in Falmouth which arrives in St Mawes Harbour. If coming by car, take the King Harry Ferry from Feock. For this route, take the A39 from Truro and at Playing Place, take the left turning marked for the ferry. Drive through Penelewey then take the second turning on the left signposted 'King Harry Ferry'. Once over the ferry, follow signs to St Mawes and park in the main car park near the harbour.

From the harbour, turn left along Lower Castle Road, past St Mawes Sailing Club and hotel, taking in the glorious view of Carrick Roads ahead. To the left is Place Manor which can be reached by a tiny foot ferry in summer months, then further round Amsterdam Point and the stretch of coastal footpath leading to St Anthony's Head and lighthouse. Continuing up Lower Castle Road, the Tresanton Hotel looms up on the right and looking out to sea this part of the Carrick Roads is always busy with boats of all kind and is where the popular TV series *Poldark* was filmed.

At the top of the hill take time to explore St Mawes Castle with its fine views over Falmouth, the docks, the Carrick Roads and if lucky, the

St Mawes Harbour

St Mawes Castle

famous Falmouth 'working boats' (oyster fishing boats) may be seen with their colourful racing colours.

Leaving the castle behind, continue down Castle Drive and along what is known locally as Millionaire's Row. These Hollywood style mansions have expansive landscaped gardens, some have huge metal gates, and an array of flowers growing from the walls: bursts of pinks in many shades; hebe and clouds of red and white valerian. At the end of the road turn right, through a five barred gate into the National Trust land of Newton Cliff. Passing a sign indicating 'St Just 1¾ miles ahead', continue along a path through fields of waist high grass with sorrel, ferns, buttercups and cow parsley.

Looking out to the left, huge tankers are often moored up in the river and a variety of sailing boats are always sailing past. After about fifteen minutes come to another high hedge: take the steep path up on the right which curves round to the right. Gorse grows to tree size here, towering above the path as it becomes even steeper, but at the top stop to catch your breath and look back down on the fabulous views over Mylor Harbour, Restronguet and Loe Beach.

Reaching a waymark post, turn left up the hill to a five barred gate and climb over a stile with Newton Farm buildings on the right. Further on is a sewage plant on the right (rather strong smelling in the heat!), and continue along a rough path until reaching Upper Cliff Road. Turn right here, past Lamorran Gardens on the left. Peeping through the trees here is a stunning view of Place Manor, then further round Carricknath Point and St Anthony lighthouse.

Passing the Tresanton Car Park on the right, round the bend where there is a small park on the left with carefully positioned benches, ideal for sitting and drinking in the view. From here, take the road back to the left, and return to St Mawes where there are no shortage of eateries including an excellent delicatessen in the arcade, where they will make up sandwiches for you to take away.

Other local places of interest

St Mawes Sailing Club **www.stmawessailing.co.uk**
St Mawes Castle **www.english-heritage.org.uk/server/show/nav.11392**
Lamorran Gardens open Mon, Wed and Fri, April - September 10-5

15. Maenporth

Taking in Maenporth beach, woodlands, and a secluded hamlet

The cove of Maenporth faces east across Falmouth Bay looking out over Pendennis Castle and St Anthony Head lighthouse. Maenporth is a fabulous beach. It's long – huge if the tide is out – and in summer it's great for swimming with young children or nervous swimmers as it's very shallow. There are also public toilets here. To one side of the beach is Maenporth café, good for ice creams and snacks, but if you want something fancier, The Cove opposite can supply you with upmarket variations, a licence and its own car park. On 30 December 1978, the Scottish trawler 'Ben Asdale' was wrecked off Maenporth – the remains can still be seen on the rocks. This walk was done in autumn.

Distance	1½ miles
Time	1 hour including a run on Maenporth beach
Terrain	One steep hill, can be very muddy
Refreshments	The Cove, Maenporth Beach Café
Map	OS Explorer 103 The Lizard, Falmouth and Helston

The Walk

From Falmouth, follow signs to Swanpool beach and continue around the coast to Maenporth which is where the walk starts. You can park on the beach but in summer you have to pay (£3 at time of writing); from late October to Easter there is currently no charge.

From the beach, cross the road taking a public footpath sign to the left of The Cove, next to a field where boats are laid up, and this path leads down an unmade drive. On the right is dense woodland; to the left an overgrown stream. It's secluded down here, and the site was derelict for years: only the shell of a house remained among an orchard with gnarled apple trees growing in a wilderness of marsh and reed.

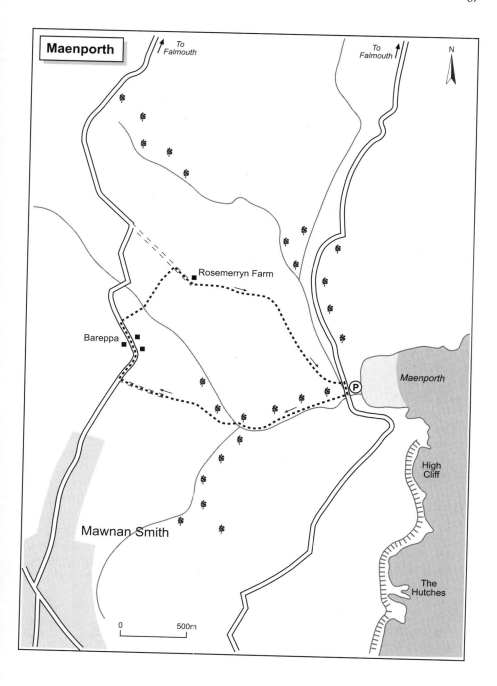

Several years ago a large, modern looking house was built called 'Maenvale'. Walk past the house along a muddy path that curves round, over a stream and a granite stile and up past fields on the right, to a steep boggy track that leads steeply uphill. This is known as Fine and Brave Lane and was an old pony or mule track used to transport seaweed, sand and lime from the limekiln at Maenporth to the fields inland. According to legend, during the French wars, the women of Mawnan saw an incoming ship and hurtled down this lane carrying pitchforks to repel an invasion. The crew saw glimpses of their red petticoats and thought the Redcoats were en route, so the ship beat a hasty retreat.

It's not difficult to imagine mutinous women storming down this track. The banks are high on each side, covered in moss and ivy, with tree roots erupting at sinewy angles. In summer sunlight peeps shyly over the hedges while sun-drunk flies buzz in loopy circles.

Climbing to the top of this hill, you come to a road: turn right into the hamlet of Bareppa which once housed miners from the nearby arsenic mine. More recently, Bareppa boasted four peacocks that would fly from the top of one cottage, over the road and land on another one, before settling next door. Rare geese and ducks used to live in one of the gardens, and it was a joy to lean over the fence to watch peacocks sheltering in their lofty treehouse, see geese and ducks parading round the lawn before swimming in their personal pond.

Walking round the corner you will come to a bench with a small placard which says: 'Mary's seat. Come rest awhile'. If you do so, listen to the steady splashing of a stream, submerged by Dr Who-like umbrellas of gunnera. The whine of a distant chainsaw, and a dog barking next door.

Getting up, look over at Bareppa House, with stone pineapples on the gateposts. This house once was home to packet ship captains whose ships carried mail from Falmouth overseas. Just past this elegant mansion is a house on the left with tiny sash windows that open sideways. Continue past this until reaching another public footpath sign on the right that leads over a granite stile and into a long field with horses next door.

This meadow leads down to another stile at the end, over a fast running stream, and into a huge field that in spring is usually bursting with sunny daffodils. Climb up the right hand circumference of the steep field and

Stile heading into a field, Bareppa

Maenporth beach

over another stile in the hedge that leads into a path that veers round to the left. Here are huge disembodied tree trunks, abandoned like fallen giants, and huge holly-type bushes with vehement prickles.

This path bears round to a five barred gate – go through this and walk opposite, following a wooden sign saying 'Footpath' and an arrow pointing to the right, past the perimeter of a large house and garden, fenced off from the public. The grand house, which looks like the set for a period drama, is set back from the path, hiding behind two sets of wrought iron gates; one set propped open, the larger ones locked shut.

Follow the path round, past the fabulous garden where glossy green lawns merge with sculptured trees, like gracious senior citizens. This path curves round to the right, through another gate – turn right here up a lane leading to the farm and turn left at the top into another field.

This looks out over Tregedna Farm and campsite with a tapestry of surrounding fields. Through another gate, enter a leafy lane where sunlight shimmers on rustling leaves and dried tendrils swing like the husks of dreadlocks. Pass through two more five barred gates and at the second look down to the left to a huge pond where three enormous white geese mingle with several families of ducks. At feeding time the birds squawk and waddle down to the water while at the other end of the field, in contrast to the bustle of feeding time, is often a single grey heron, statue-still save for the ruffling of its tail feathers.

Head down the hill towards the sea. A few minutes later cross the road and you are back on Maenporth beach.

16. Carwinion Walk, Mawnan Smith

A circular walk popular with local dogwalkers encompassing woods, fields and the coastal footpath

Carwinion House is a beautiful 18th Century stone manor house tucked away in its own private estate in this lush North Helford area of Cornwall. The beautiful gardens are open to the public, and Jane Roger's cream teas, served on Carwinion's garden terrace, are thought by some to be the best in Cornwall and have to be sampled to be believed. Carwinion is dog friendly and welcomes visitors throughout the year. This walk was done on a hot day in July.

Helford River

The Walk

From Falmouth drive through Swanpool and Maenporth towards Mawnan Smith. Passing a sign saying Woodlands on the left, continue round the corner and park next to Carwinion Playing Fields, opposite Carwinion Garden, famous for its bamboos and cream teas. To the right of the

Distance	2¼ miles returning the inland route; 2½ miles returning via the coastal footpath
Time	1½ hours
Terrain	Moderate, steep in places
Refreshments	Mrs Jane Rogers, Carwinion House, Carwinion Road, Mawnan Smith, Falmouth, Cornwall, England, TR11 5JA Phone: 01326 250258 Email: jane@carwinion.co.uk
Maps	OS Landranger 204 Truro and Falmouth Roseland Peninsula and OS Explorer 103 The Lizard Falmouth and Helston

garden a public footpath sign marks the start of the walk: go down a rocky lane that leads into dense woods by the side of Carwinion Garden. The going is rough here and in wet weather can be slippery, but further on the path becomes well trodden earth and is kinder to the feet, while huge ferns tower above.

At a fork in the steep path through this wooded valley take the left hand turning over a small slate bridge, past an unexpected burst of orange montbretia, and head further down into the woods where the incline levels out. A stream splashes beside on the left and overhead you can sometimes hear the cry of a buzzard or the tapping of a woodpecker.

The path finally levels out into Bosloe Meadows. Continue through another gate and down to a pebbled cove especially popular with dog walkers, as this private beach is dog friendly all year round. According to the map it is Porth Saxon, but known locally as Porth Sawsen.

Continue along the path to the left of the beach, and head up the hill, past a boathouse and over a stile into another field, through a kissing gate that is often waterlogged in winter and down to Porthallack Cove – otherwise known as Cow Beach or Church Cove.

Jumping over a stream edged with wild bamboos, there is an overgrown gate on the left with a sign saying 'Mawnan Old Church ½ mile, Mawnan Smith 1½ miles'. If you wish to take the slightly shorter, inland route, go through this gate which will take you through several fields to Mawnan

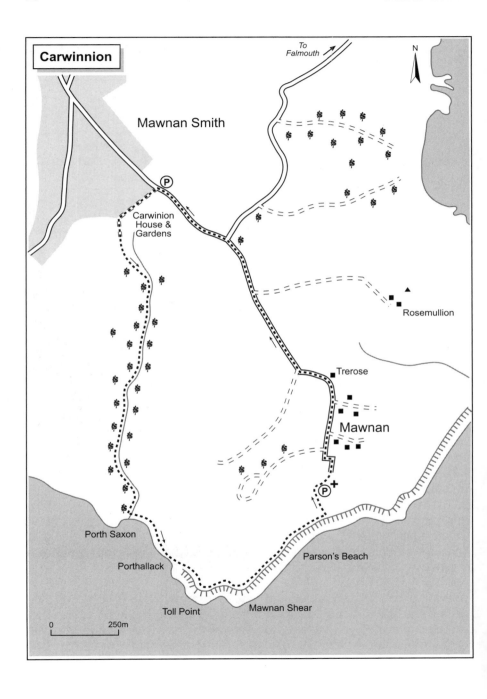

Carwinnion

Mawnan Smith

To Falmouth

N

Carwinion House & Gardens

Rosemullion

Trerose

Mawnan

Porth Saxon

Porthallack

Parson's Beach

Toll Point

Mawnan Shear

0   250m

Church, then along the road and turn left at the Catholic church back to Carwinion. But note that there are often cattle in this field so keep dogs on a lead.

For the slightly longer route, continue along the path through a gate and up an incredibly steep field that leads to the coastal footpath. Pause at the top of this field to look back over stunning views of the Helford river, of Trebah Gardens and Durgan beach. In summer, sailors in small boats enjoy the excellent sailing round here, while some moor off coves only approachable by water, *Swallows and Amazons* style.

Pass through a new gate which leads to the coastal footpath which is steep and usually sheltered from the wind. Look down onto the Helford river down below and you can often think you're in Greece: the waters around here are usually clear and aquamarine, where seals and cormorants can often be seen.

On the opposite shore lies St Anthony's, Denis Head, and the far peninsula of Nare Point. The footpath ends in another stile leading to a field where there are often cattle. Head across the field into dense woods with a carpet of crunchy leaves, where the sea

Mawnan Church

glints through slender trunks dappled with sunlight. Taking the path to the left, scramble over another stile and reach Mawnan Parish Church, which is well worth a visit.

The church is a navigational aid to boats entering the river and it seems that a cruciform building was erected in the 13th century, though there are 14th century windows and the north and part of the south aisle were added in the 15th century. It is a beautiful building, popular for weddings, and the arch above the church door is often decorated with garlands of orange and white flowers, white ribbons and white roses.

Mawnan churchyard is especially graceful: the ground is soft and mossy, the grass mown lovingly. Ancient gravestones lean, smothered in beards of grey lichen, entwined with the occasional bramble. The sea is just visible through the trees, and there is a quiet stillness here, a sense of peace. A perfect resting place.

Walk out through the car park and take the only road out for a walk along the quiet country lane back towards Mawnan Smith. Along the way pass noisy sparrows darting above a bank of wild pink roses sprawling in and around a tree. Continue on past the Catholic church where the road forks, and take the left turning back towards Carwinion and the car.

Looking up the valley from Porth Sawsen

17. Frenchman's Creek
A walk in Du Maurier country

Daphne Du Maurier's 'Frenchman's Creek' was inspired by the pirates and free traders who worked these waters during the Napoleonic wars. Long ago Helford was an important port where trading ships brought rum, port, tobacco and lace from the continent. Those days are long gone, the houses mostly holiday homes, but Du Maurier's descriptions of the Helford river are so vivid, you can still identify this magical, secretive part of Cornwall. This walk was done on a brilliant summer's day.

Distance	3 miles
Time	2 hours
Terrain	Steep at times
Helford ferry	Check seasonal running times on www.helford-river-boats.co.uk/ferry or ring 01326 250770
Parking	£1 all day at time of walking
Refreshments	Ferryboat Inn, Shipwrights Inn. Post office and shop at Helford Village
Map	OS Explorer 103 The Lizard, Falmouth and Helston

The Walk

From Falmouth take the road to Mawnan Smith. In the village follow signs to Glendurgan and Trebah Gardens, then on to the Ferryboat Inn. Nearing the bottom of the hill is a car park on the right where you can park all day. Walk the remainder of the way down to Helford Passage and wait for the passenger ferry (£5 return for adults at time of walking) on the beach outside the Ferryboat Inn.

The ferry travels to Helford Point opposite, where the path leads to Helford Village and past the picturesque Shipwrights Inn which is closed

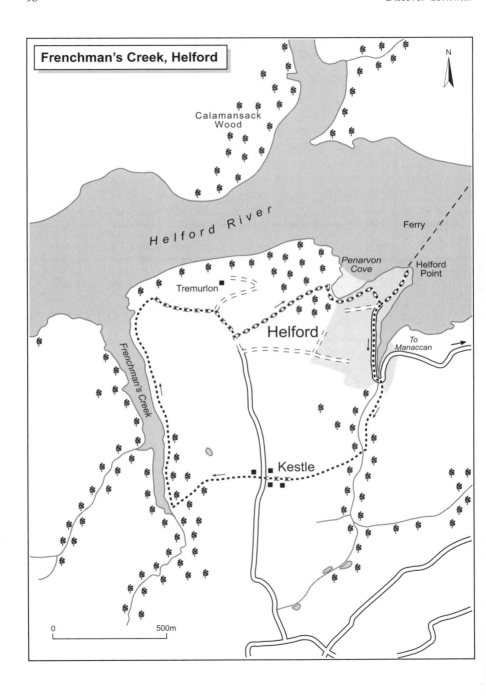

Looking up the Helford River to Groyne Point

from 2.30 till 6pm so don't try to go there in the afternoon. Continue over a footbridge and on reaching a row of whitewashed cottages, turn right by a public footpath sign saying 'Manaccan ¾ miles'. After a short distance the lane continues past a thatched cottage and into woods where the sun dances through the trees, dappling the leaves with an intense white light.

Follow the path as it forks right over a stream, go over a small granite stile up through the woods and into a field. At the top of this field climb over a stile signed 'Alternative Permissive Footpath' and into another field to the left of Kestle Farm. At the end of this field is a sign on the right to Frenchman's Creek – follow that through a gate onto the main road. A few yards further on take the public footpath sign on the left which leads to another path by the side of a field with a hedge of bay trees, looking out over lush green fields.

Passing through a wooden gate pass a seat made of a huge slab of granite, with orchards on the right and head down into more woodland. The rough lane has diagonal stones acting as gullies to channel the water that must run through the woods – a sensible precaution in these times of abundant rain. Pass a huge old oak tree with the trunk split in half, smothered in thick moss; further up its ivy coated branches, bracken sprouts like tufts of hair.

Coming to a fork in the path follow a sign indicating 'Frenchman's Creek (Permissive Path)' and head even further downhill to the water. Frenchman's Creek is a secretive, silent place, ingrained with the sense of times gone by. At low tide the creek is littered with rotting trees, draped in seaweed; a lone egret may stalk through a mud bank while rooks caw above. Follow the path alongside the creek, pass over three footbridges, and by a tree on the left, take the right fork which leads up some steps. Follow the Creekside Path which does just that, passing round the end of the creek, where there is a wonderful view of the two old quays of traditional Cornish stone, the Helford river ahead, and the final resting place of an old shipwrecked boat. Out in the open inhale the toasty smell of sun baked bracken and continue until reaching a tarmac path – headed right uphill with a field on the left.

Frenchman's Creek

Looking across from Helford to Helford Passage

At the top of this steep hill is a conveniently placed bench and a good spot for one last look back across Helford River. Turn right along a track signed Penarvon Cove, cross a submerged cattle grid and turn left signed to Pengwedhen and Helford.

Heading down this lane pass another tree covered in bouncy ivy, like an afro hairstyle. Coming to a fork, continue downhill until reaching the idyllic Penarvon Cove. From here take the public footpath sign back through the woods, climbing away from the cove, through a metal gate at the top, and continue until reaching a steep path that leads downhill to the left, back into Helford Village, by the Shipwrights Inn.

From here turn left to get the passenger ferry back to Helford Passage.

18. Sennen Cove and Gwynver

A walk at one of Cornwall's most famous surfing beaches – "the bay where dolphins play"

Sennen Cove is the most westerly village in England and Sennen Cove's white sands have ensured that it is one of Cornwall's best beaches, attracting families and surfers alike. It is also home to Bilbo, Britain's first fully trained canine lifeguard!

Cape Cornwall's distinctive mining chimney can be seen across the bay and come here as the sun sets and you will never forget the sight. The walk follows the coastal path round Whitesand Bay to Gwynver Beach (pronounced Gwenver) then inland paths provide the return route.

Distance	4 miles
Time	2 hours
Terrain	Very steep in parts
Refreshments	Various cafés in Sennen Cove; Old Success Inn, Phone 01736 871232
Map	OS Explorer 102 Lands End, Penzance and St Ives

The Walk

Take the A30 from Penzance towards Lands End and turn right to Sennen Cove, parking in the large car park at the bottom of the hill which cost £2.70 for 3 hours at time of walking.

At the far end of the car park, find a yellow waymark sign next to another sign saying 'No Camping Private Property', and turn left to follow a sandy path parallel to Sennen Cove.

At a split in the path carry straight on, admiring the waves that crash along the almost white sands of the beach, and the black suited surfers bobbing up and down like seals. Across the bay can be seen the headland of Cape Cornwall with its distinctive mining chimney, and on the right,

Gwynver Beach

high above, loom several Martello towers used as lookout stations in the Second World War.

Passing a lifeguard station below on the left, continue towards some cottages and take the next left down a steep sandy path to the beach. Cross a trickle of a stream and head towards a large yellow sign in the sand dunes saying 'Telephone Cable', up some steep sandy steps to a path and turn left.

After a concrete bunker, find a more defined coastal path and continue parallel to the beach, with huge granite slabs set in moorland on the right. Following the granite studded footpath, look down on Gwynver Beach before taking a slight right fork uphill.

Reaching a long flight of steps, climb up a steep path with laurel bushes on either side.

Continue walking until reaching a fork and turn right, past a sign saying 'Kingshill Bed and Breakfast', and walk down a track with chicken runs on

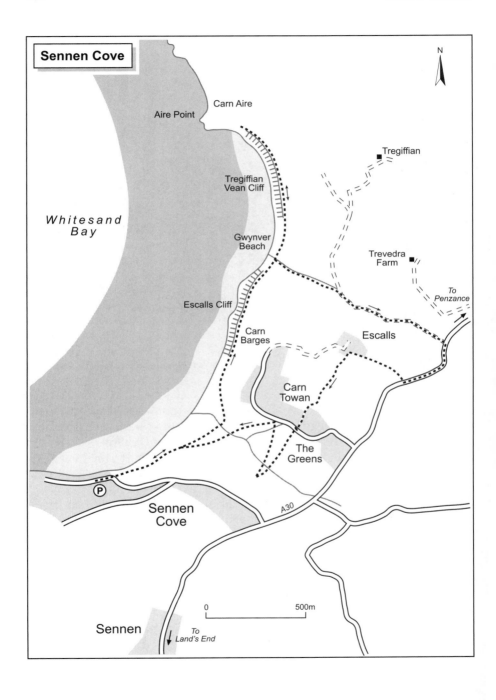

one side. Along another path, look out over the tumbling waves of Whitesand Bay. Walking on, come to more houses and a tarmac lane which winds round through the houses and finally – after about half a mile – find a public footpath sign on the right largely obscured by foliage.

Head down a steep, sandy footpath towards more cottages and follow the path in between the first and second cottages nearest the sea which leads to the earlier path you walk in on. Further on, reach a wooden bridge over a stream next to what were presumably fishermen's cottages nestling in the sand dunes, sympathetically restored.

From here the sandy path continues back to Sennen where the Roundhouse Gallery and Old Success Inn are both worth a visit.

Sennen harbour

19. Carn Euny and Chapel Carn Brea

A walk in Penwith taking in a Neolithic village and the most westerly hill in Britain

The ancient village of Carn Euny has evidence of Iron Age and post-Iron Age settlements going back to the Neolithic period. The huts were excavated in the 1960s and have been rebuilt over time, with each house linking to the next one. These timber huts, only found in West Cornwall, were built around 200 BC, but by the first century BC, were replaced by stone huts, lived in by farmers, tin dealers and stockbreeders. They farmed about 40 acres around the village of oats, barley and rye.

Carn Euny is well known for its large underground passageway or fogou (Cornish for cave) which was possibly used for storage, living or ritual. The site is well preserved, over 20 metres long and runs just underneath the ground, and is roofed by huge stone slabs. It was abandoned late in the Roman period, and was dug out in 2010 when heavy rain flooded it. This walk was done in October.

Carn Euny

Distance	3 miles
Time	2 hours
Terrain	Can be very muddy
Refreshments	None
Map	OS Explorer 102 Lands End, Penzance and St Ives

The Walk

Leaving Penzance, take the A30 towards Land's End and at the village of Drift turn right following the brown heritage signs to Carn Euny. The lane twists and turns, through high walled hedges and remote moorland, for about 3 miles when there is an almost hidden sign to Carn Euny. Go up a steep track until reaching what looks like someone's garden. Round to the left is a small car park hidden in the trees and another sign to Carn Euny.

This stony track leads past a cottage overwhelmed by hydrangea-filled undergrowth, then further up is an assortment of elderly vans and jeeps, long abandoned, festooned with spare car bonnets. Climb over a granite stile and into a field. Further up is a painted sign to Carn Euny on the left, flanked by two huge granite gate posts.

The Fogou

From here it is a short walk into the ancient village where you will find maps and information at various points, as well as stunning views over Penwith. Just below the sign to the fogou is a dark little lane leading off to the right: walk round the back of a cottage on the left and continue until reaching a fork where a barn was being rebuilt. Turn right here, then immediately left, where the path can be extremely muddy.

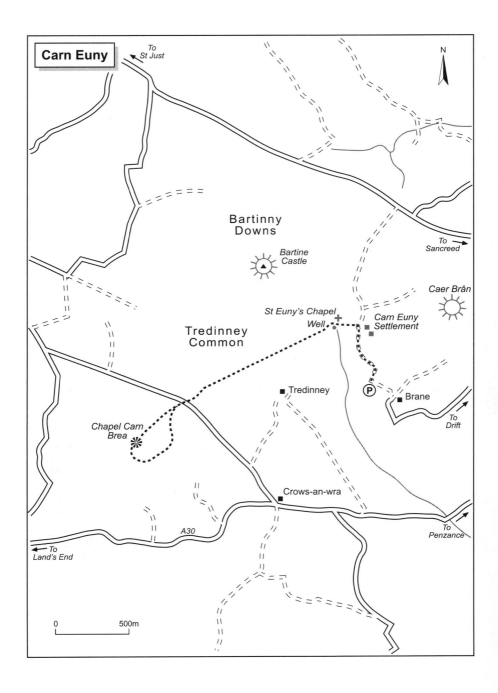

Looming ahead is Carn Euny Well. Hung from trees nearby were festooned all kinds of 'cloutie' – strips of rag, a key, a scarf, the letter Z and a teddy bear. Legend has it that if you wish to be healed by St. Euny's Well, "you must come and wash upon the three first Wednesdays in May". Another method of healing is to tie something that had been in contact with the affected part to a tree: as the rag rots, the illness should pass away.

This path is thick with well trodden mud and, judging by the plentiful hoof marks, popular with riders as well as walkers. Walking along, there is the most fabulous view over the moorland. Gorse was in flower here, the last of the blackberries, and bracken, toasted a crackly brown by the summer. To the right is a quarry where skylarks sing over Bartinney Downs.

At the end of this track, cross the road and turn right, then immediately left. Walk through a car park to see Chapel Carn Brea which is the most westerly hill in Britain and where a beacon is lit every Midsummer's eve. The hill is 657 feet above sea level and looking out to the horizon we counted three layers of blue, where it met the skyline.

Tredinney Common from Chapel Carn Brea

Climbing a steep dry path to the summit affords fabulous views: distant waves break off Longships, then further round to Stone's Reef. St Just lies to the north, Sennen and Lands End to the west, and Mounts Bay to the southeast. Land's End Aerodrome is nearby, distinguished by a red wind sock and tiny planes that buzzed above like friendly bees.

Following the OS map, there is a slightly different route back to Carn Euny, or retrace the route back the way you have come.

There is a Bronze age Chambered Barrow at the summit of Chapel Carn Brea, and the site of a medieval chapel.

20. Church Cove

A walk on the west coast of the Lizard Peninsula, taking in Church Cove, Mullion Golf Course and Poldhu Cove

"Lizard" in this context derives from the Cornish "lis" meaning "place" and "ard" meaning "high" and refers to the whole of this peninsula including the most southerly village in England. But the connection with reptiles comes from the famous Serpentine rock local to this area, which looks like snakeskin when polished.

Poldhu, meaning black cove in Cornish, is better known for the Poldhu Wireless Station, where Marconi transmitted the first transatlantic radio message on December 12, 1901 to a receiving station in St John's, Newfoundland. In 1923 and 1924, Marconi used Poldhu again for shortwave radio experiments, resulting in the development of the Beam Wireless Service for the British Post Office.

Poldhu station continued to operate until 1933. The site was cleared in 1935 and six acres were given to the National Trust in 1937 with the rest of the site added in 1960. In 2001 the Marconi Centre, a new museum/meeting building, was opened nearby. This walk was done on a cold day in November.

Distance	3½ miles
Time	1 - 1½ hours
Terrain	Easy, but muddy at times
Facilities	Public toilets near Winnianton Farm and car park
Car Park	National Trust car park: £1 per day at time of walking
Refreshments	Halzephron Inn or beach café near Church Cove (summer only)
Maps	OS Explorer 103 The Lizard or National Trust Lizard West Coast leaflet

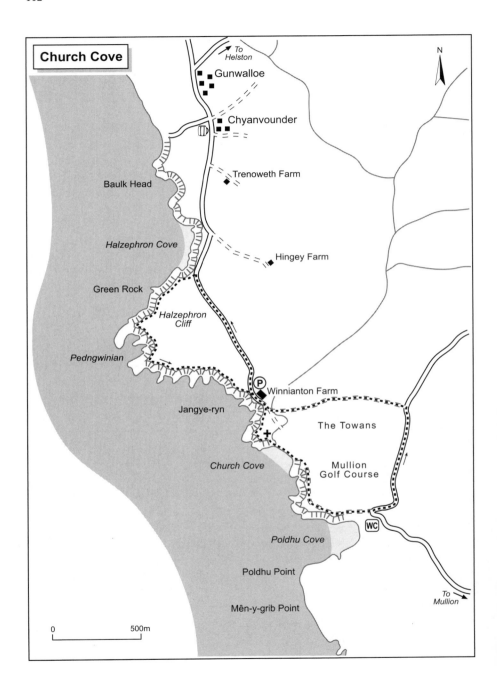

Church Cove

To Helston

Gunwalloe

Chyanvounder

Trenoweth Farm

Baulk Head

Halzephron Cove

Hingey Farm

Green Rock

Halzephron Cliff

Pedngwinian

Winnianton Farm

Jangye-ryn

The Towans

Mullion Golf Course

Church Cove

Poldhu Cove

Poldhu Point

WC

To Mullion

Mên-y-grib Point

N

0   500m

The Walk

Travel south from Helston past Culdrose airbase and turn right, taking signs for Gunwalloe. Heading towards Church Cove, park in a National Trust pay and display car park near Winnianton Farm.

On foot, head back up the road where the lane leads steeply upwards, past an austere granite house which could have been the old rectory, with a moss encrusted roof, empty windows and towering narrow chimneys. The hedges are spiky, with gnarled and weather beaten branches, filled with an odd assortment of vegetation: a burst of honeysuckle in amongst the brambles; the bright buds of rosehips; teasel, like skinny hedgehogs with spindly arms.

At a layby at the top of the hill turn right onto the coastal footpath, heading south towards Halzephron Cliffs – so called because "als" means Hell in Cornish, and "ephron" comes from the Cornish "yfarn" for cliff. If you look down at the rocks far below you can see why it got its name.

This path is narrow and can be very muddy, but looking out over Mounts Bay the view is magnificent: a massive sweep of sea, majestic in a slate

Church Cove

blue robe with ermine waves. Down the coast Mousehole and Lamorna are visible, then on to Gwennap Head, and beyond that Land's End.

The waves rumble far below and seagulls gather on the rocks like white studs, while their mates cry and wheel above.

Walking round the headland is an ornate and magnificent white building which looks like a James Bond style hotel but was originally the Poldhu Hotel, built for Marconi workers, and is now a care home. Heading further south, Goonhilly can be seen in the distance.

Climbing down, the path leads to Jangye-ryn, a rough beach with rock formations of special interest to geologists because the contorted strata of the cliffs represent 1,000s of years of tectonic movement. It is otherwise known as Dollar Cove, because a Spanish ship was apparently wrecked here in the 17th century and silver dollars occasionally wash up on the beach.

Statue at Church Cove

Church Cove is separated from this beach by a 60 foot promontory that provides a good view of both beaches and the church of St Winwalloe. Apparently there was a church and settlement here in Domesday times, though the current church was built in 14th or 15th century and the tower is Norman. St Winwalloe's is unusual in that its small tower nestles in the inner bank of this headland, separate from the adjoining main body of the church and ancient graveyard. Another unusual aspect is its proximity to the beach – at spring tides with high winds, the spray must drench the front door.

St Winwalloe was of Cornish parentage, born in Brittany in the sixth century. There's a figure of him by the porch, a Cornish cross in the churchyard, and the church contains timbers from the Portuguese galleon *St Anthony,* which was wrecked in the cove on Saturday, 19 January, 1527.

This cove is dangerous and breathtaking: you can understand why so many ships were wrecked on this coast. Visiting here one Christmas Day I saw brave swimmers struggle out from the pounding surf to be rewarded with hot toddies by a bonfire.

From the cove, head off towards the public toilets and café and turn left to cross a small bridge over the National Trust Towans or golf course. You might have to wait for golfers to complete their shots as you walk over the golf course, but after a while pass Mullion Golf Club and take the lane south which leads down to Poldhu Cove, famous for being the place where the first transatlantic radio signal was sent in 1901. There is a café here but it is closed in winter. Head north, back to Church Cove. Some of this rocky path has been dangerously eroded and rerouted inland, pinpointed by signs saying 'Warning! Unstable Cliffs'.

Follow the path back down to Church Cove, then continue back up the lane, past the toilet block and café, to the National Trust car park.

Note
Dogs banned on Church Cove from Easter to 1st October 1st. Dogs are allowed year round on adjoining Dollar Cove.

Other local places of interest
15th century St Winwalloe church, built in the sand dunes on the beach.

Also from Sigma:

Cornwall Walking on the level
Norman & June Buckley

This seventh volume extends the Sigma 'Level Walk' series to Cornwall, a county of great walking potential, but with so many of the popular areas needing the ability to tackle prolonged and steep climbs, particularly along the South West Coast Path. This book selects and illustrates 28 routes, mainly circular, which explore some of the finest parts of the county, without serious ascent. In addition to the route directions, the distance, ascent, car parking, refreshment and map, with a succinct assessment, are provided for each walk.
£8.99

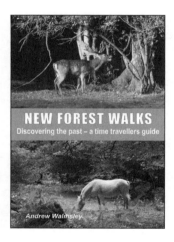

New Forest Walks
Discovering the Past – a time travellers guide
Andrew Walmsley

Explore the New Forest with this series of 16 walks through ancient landscapes where long-forgotten bumps, hollows and moss-clad earthen banks have stories to tell of Bronze and Iron Age peoples, Romans, Normans and others who lived, worked and hunted here. Illustrated throughout with colour photographs.
£12.99

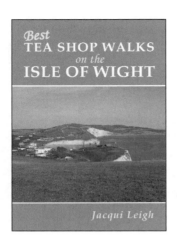

Best Tea Shop Walks on the Isle of Wight
Jacqui Leigh

The Isle of Wight is a wonderful place to walk with 500 miles of footpaths, the highest footpath density in the UK, and numerous teashops in beautiful locations. The walks in this book vary in length and difficulty; some include at least part suitable for wheelchair users or pushchairs, giving the option of 'there and back' walks. The teashops range from the very tradition to modern cafe style establishments and some operate as licenced restaurants.
£8.99

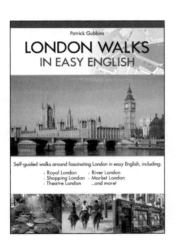

London Walks in Easy English
Patrick Gubbins

Forget the boring "walk books" that take you down quiet streets where nothing happens. *London Walks in Easy English* knows where the busy, exciting places in the capital are, and makes sure you see London life with all its colour, tradition, food, views, art, beautiful buildings and, most importantly, its sense of fun.

What other book of walks takes you inside the classrooms of London University, into courtrooms to see real trials in progress, into shops to try exotic food, and to the big attractions but also to many other fascinating places that even Londoners don't know?

London Walks in Easy English takes you through the capital's busiest and liveliest areas, with easy-to-follow walks in conversational-level English.
£9.99

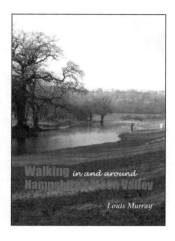

Walking in and around Hampshire's Meon Valley
Louis Murray

The river Meon is one of Hampshire's quintessential chalk streams. It rises from natural springs in the South Downs to the south of the village of East Meon. This book contains the details of 20 walks in the Meon river valley area in southern Hampshire. The walks are suitable for novices, casual walkers, family groups, and experienced ramblers.

£8.99

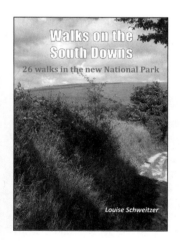

Walks on the South Downs
26 in the new National Park
Louise Shweitzer

Twenty five circular trails range from five to ten miles long around some of the most unspoilt and spectacular scenery in England on waymarked public footpaths, bridleways, old coach roads and an occasional tarmac lane. Most routes feature a particular landmark, viewpoint, monument or preserved antiquity, touching the more familiar long distance trails in passing, but creating new viewpoints for the present from some perspectives of the past.

£8.99

Waterside Walking in the Peak District
Keith Stevens

30 great family walks around the Derbyshire Peak District, centred on rivers, reservoirs and canals. A fascinating insight into how the various water features operate and evolve, combined with stunning scenery and interesting landmarks. A complete walking experience.

The walks visit all the major water features in the Peak District, organised into five areas, with clear instructions on travel as well on the walk route itself. Once completed, the reader will have enjoyed and understood the key aspects of how rivers (with mills, weirs and underground caverns) shape the landscape, how the canals were built and supplied with water, and how our drinking water reservoirs are managed.

£8.99

Family Walks in East Cheshire
Jean Warham

25 walks, all circular and about 3 to 4 miles long. They are never too steep or difficult, and can be walked at an easy pace in about one and a half to two hours, allowing time to admire the view or look at the birds or wild flowers along the way. They are all chosen for their variety of scenery, including particular places of beauty or interest.

£8.99

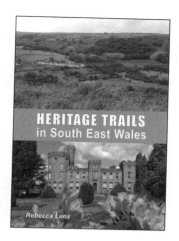

Heritage Walks in South East Wales
Rebecca Lees

A collection of trails exploring the history of South East Wales, from prehistoric times to beyond the Industrial Revolution. The trails range from short to strenuous and include town trails and countryside terrain.

The 20 walks are diverse in length and landscape, yet they all have one thing in common; the rich history of south east Wales. From the world-class Blaenavon Heritage Site at the uppermost tip of the south Wales coalfields to the sweeping expanse of Cardiff Bay, the trails are centred on the vibrancy of Wales' past, with the aim of bringing back to life some of her most notable events and characters.

£8.99

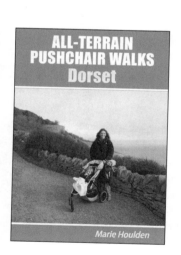

All-Terrain Pushchair Walks Dorset
Marie Houlden

Situated at the very South of England, Dorset benefits from magnificent coast lines, beautiful country parks, stunning areas of natural beauty and history and wildlife in abundance. The 25 walks will allow the reader to experience amazing views, historic sites, fascinating and quaint market towns and gain information on accessible family attractions. The walks vary the length, coving mixture of terrains and different types of environment, so that there is something for everyone.

£8.99

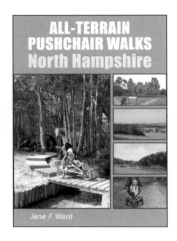

All-Terrain Pushchair Walks
North Hampshire
Jane F Ward

30 carefully selected all-terrain buggy walks in beautiful North Hampshire. From strolls through ancient forests, heathland rambles to spectacular uplands romps. Whether you're walking to keep fit or to enjoy the great outdoors.
£8.99

Discovering Manchester
2nd Edition
Barry Worthington

This stylish walking guide doubles as a detailed account of the city's architecture, its history and tourism attractions. There are walks throughout Manchester including such major entertainment and cultural centres as the Bridgewater Hall, Urbis, the Museum of Science and Industry, the Lowry and many more. Explore the entire city – from the Corn Exchange to G-Mex, from the Cathedral to Affleck's Palace.
£10.99

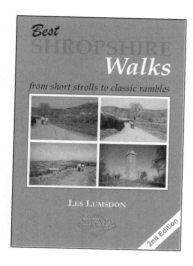

Best Shropshire Walks
2nd Edition
From short strolls to classic rambles
Les Lumsdon

A new revised edition of this much loved guide contains 36 walks, including 12 completely new routes, located in all parts of the county. Several walks feature fine hill walking on the Welsh borders and others start from delightful villages and hamlets in the north and east of the county.
£8.99

Exploring the North Peak & South Pennines
25 rollercoaster mountain bike rides
Michael Ely

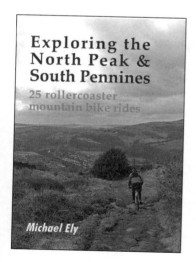

This book will inspire you to pump up the tyres and oil the chain for some excitement, exercise and a feast of rollercoaster riding as you join Michael Ely on some great mountain biking in these Pennine hills. Over 500 miles of riding for the adventurous off-road cyclist that explore the tracks and steep lanes in the Pennine hills. There are twenty-five illustrated rides - with cafe stops half way round - to provide both a challenge and many hours of healthy exercise in classic mountain biking country.
£8.99

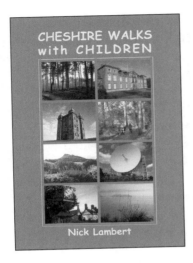

Cheshire Walks With Children 2nd Edition
Nick Lambert

Now completely revised and updated, this was the first in our "walks with children" series and has quickly become a firm favourite. There are 30 walks, ranging in length, together with things to look out for and questions to answer along the way make it an entertaining book for young and old alike.

£8.99

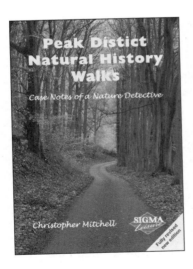

Peak District Walking Natural History Walks
Christopher Mitchell

An updated 2nd Edition with 18 varied walks for all lovers of the great outdoors — and armchair ramblers too! Learn how to be a nature detective, a 'case notes' approach shows you what clues to look for and how to solve them. Detailed maps include animal tracks and signs, landscape features and everything you need for the perfect natural history walk. There are mysteries and puzzles to solve to add more fun for family walks — solutions supplied! Includes follow on material with an extensive Bibliography and 'Taking it Further' sections.

£8.99

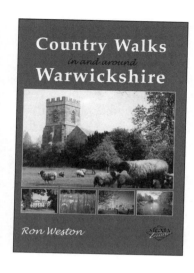

Country Walks in and around Warwickshire
Ron Weston

This selection of 32 Warwickshire walks takes you on a journey of picturesque villages and historic churches, stately homes and castles, famous gardens and medieval tracks bound together by a superb network of public footpaths and canal towpaths and sometimes spilling over into adjoining counties. All walks in the book are circular, the longest being 5.5 miles and all within a radius of 25 miles from Coventry, with directions of how to get there and where to park.

£8.99

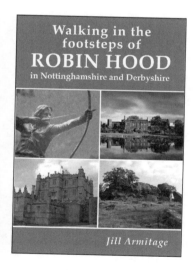

Walking in the footsteps of Robin Hood
in Nottinghamshire and Derbyshire
Jill Armitage

Walking in the Footsteps of Robin Hood roots out the places mentioned in traditional old tales and visits the locations that Robin and his men would have known. Walk through some of middle England's finest countryside on miles of well-marked footpaths to interesting historical sites associated with the outlaw legend. Stoops, caves, wells and stones with the outlaws names have been traced and woven into the walks taking you through Robin Hood country.

£8.99

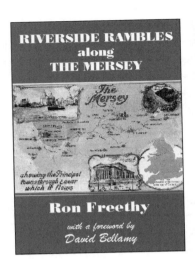

Riverside Rambles along The Mersey
Ron Freethy
with a foreword by David Bellamy

This is far more than a guidebook for walkers, it is also a portrait of one of the world's greatest rivers – once so polluted that Michael Heseltine described the state of the Mersey basin as "an affront to civilised society". Nowadays, however, salmon pass through the estuary, wildlife abounds along the entire catchment area and a rich and diverse coastline attracts a huge variety of birdlife.

Featuring 30 walks short, gentle walks (mostly circular). Explore the unique scenery, ecology and heritage of this area.
£8.99

Wirral Walks 2nd Edition
100 miles of the best walks in the area
Anthony Annakin-Smith

A completely revised and updated edition of this popular collection of 25 walks from around 2 to 10 miles, covering a total of 100 miles through the best of the local landscape. The author's careful research highlights the interesting and unusual features seen along each route.
£8.99

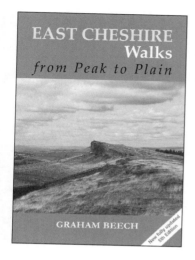

East Cheshire Walks from Peak to Plain
Graham Beech

East Cheshire is a land of contracts — from rugged hills to gently rolling countryside. Thanks to this variety, there really is something for walkers of all interests and abilities — and *East Cheshire Walks* is by far the most comprehensive guidebook to the area, with almost 40 walks ranging from 3 to 20 miles covering a total of over 250 miles. There are easy ambles in Cheshire's mid-county pasture land, interesting strolls alongside rivers and canals, and a selection of more strenuous hikes in the foothills of the Peak District.

£8.99